CHINA TO 1850

A SHORT HISTORY

CHARLES O. HUCKER

CHINA TO 1850
A SHORT HISTORY

STANFORD UNIVERSITY PRESS

STANFORD, CALIFORNIA

Stanford University Press
Stanford, California
© 1975,1976, 1978 by the Board of Trustees
of the Leland Stanford Junior University
Printed in the United States of America
Cloth ISBN 0-8047-0957-2
Paper ISBN 0-8047-0958-0
Original printing 1978
Last figure below indicates year of this printing:
00 99 98 97 96 95 94 93 92 91

PREFACE

THIS BOOK is a very simplified overview, but I believe a sound and balanced one, of how the Chinese and their culture evolved from prehistory to about 1850. It draws heavily from my more detailed work *China's Imperial Past: An Introduction to Chinese History and Culture* (1975), from which I have actually borrowed sentences, paragraphs, and even whole sections when appropriate. But this presentation, written for a quite different audience, forgoes the analytical approach to topics era by era—and, of necessity, the abundant translations and illustrations—that characterize *China's Imperial Past,* in favor of a more straightforwardly chronological, integrated treatment, an approach that seems to me most effective for this kind of short introduction to the general history of traditional Chinese civilization.

The standard modern Chinese calligraphy appearing in the text is the work of my faculty colleague Mrs. Jing-heng S. Ma; and the dragon figure on the front cover is taken from a Ch'ing dynasty porcelain plate, whose owners in New York City prefer to remain anonymous.

I owe the inspiration for this book to successive generations of students in my undergraduate classes at the University of Michigan, and I dedicate it to them and their successors.

C.O.H.

Ann Arbor
June 26, 1977

CONTENTS

CHRONOLOGY

Hsia dynasty (unverified), 2205?–1766? B.C.
Shang dynasty, 1766?–1122? B.C.
Chou dynasty, 1122?–256 B.C.
    Western Chou era, 1122?–771 B.C.
    Eastern Chou era, 770–256 B.C.
        Spring and Autumn period, 722–481 B.C.
        Warring States period, 403–221 B.C.
Ch'in dynasty, 221–206 B.C.
Han (or Former or Western Han) dynasty, 202 B.C.–A.D. 9
Hsin dynasty (usurpation of Wang Mang), A.D. 9–23
Later Han (or Eastern Han) dynasty, 25–220
Three Kingdoms era, 220–280
Chin (or Western Chin) dynasty, 266–316
Era of North-South Division, 316–589
    Sixteen Kingdoms, 301–439
    Northern and Southern Dynasties, 317–589
Sui dynasty, 581–618
T'ang dynasty, 618–907
Five Dynasties Era, 907–960
    Five Dynasties (in the north), 907–960
    Ten Kingdoms (in the south), 907–979
Sung (or Northern Sung) dynasty, 960–1127
Liao dynasty (Ch'i-tan in the north), 916–1125
Chin dynasty (Jurchen in the north), 1115–1234
Southern Sung dynasty, 1127–1279
Yüan dynasty (Mongols), 1264–1368
Ming dynasty, 1368–1644
Ch'ing dynasty (Manchus), 1644–1912
Republic of China
    On mainland, 1912–1949
    In Taiwan, 1949–
People's Republic of China, 1949–

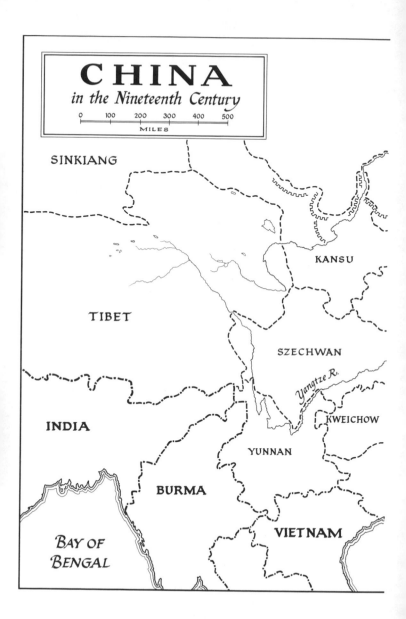

CHINA
in the Nineteenth Century

0   100   200   300   400   500
MILES

SINKIANG

KANSU

TIBET

SZECHWAN

Yangtze R.

KWEICHOW

INDIA

YUNNAN

BURMA

VIETNAM

BAY OF
BENGAL

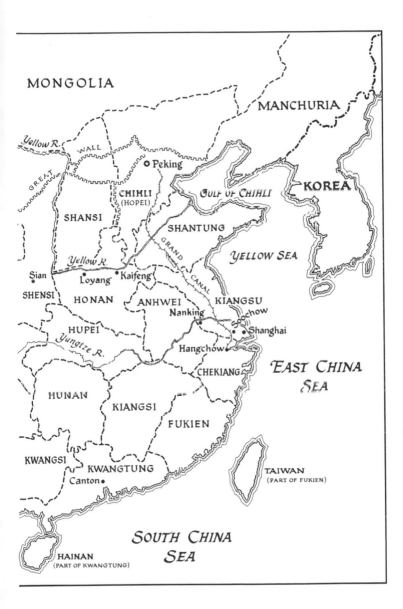

CHINA TO 1850

A SHORT HISTORY

INTRODUCTION

Westerners have been fascinated by China since the most ancient times. Romans in the age of the Caesars clamored for Chinese silk. The thirteenth-century traveler Marco Polo astonished generations of Europeans with his awed descriptions of the great cities, the vast population, and the uncountable riches of the Chinese empire. Columbus stumbled on the Americas in 1492 while trying to find a new route to China, and to Henry Hudson in the seventeenth century the lure of China was so strong that North America still seemed just a frustrating obstacle to be got through or around. Meanwhile, reports from China by Christian missionaries were being read so avidly in Europe that Confucius almost became the patron saint of the eighteenth-century Enlightenment. By the nineteenth century European and American traders, missionaries, diplomats, sailors, and soldiers had become entangled inescapably in the turbulent development of China's modern history.

Our attitudes toward China have fluctuated between admiration and revulsion, between hope and despair. At times we long to think of the hundreds of millions of Chinese as prospective customers and potential converts; at other times we shrink from the Yellow Peril. We perceive China at times as a benign Charlie Chan, at times as a malign Fu Manchu. Sometimes we just resign ourselves to the hopelessness of making sense of a country so strange that traditionally its women wore pants and its men wore gowns. But our fascination with China has seldom waned for long.

Twentieth-century Westerners, and especially Americans,

have been embroiled in a series of Asian wars that brought us into close contact with China—World War II in the 1940's, Korea in the 1950's, and Vietnam in the 1960's and 1970's. Particularly since the establishment of a communist People's Republic in mainland China in 1949, Sino-American relations have been confusing, unpredictable, and often strained. Suddenly China has emerged on the world scene as a power wielder, meddling in the affairs of distant peoples in Africa, Eastern Europe, and Cuba. In the background of foreign policy thinking throughout the Free World is the possibility of some calamitous global confrontation that might force us to choose between siding with China against Russia and siding with Russia against China.

Even if China posed no conceivable military threat to anyone, however, the study of China would still occupy many people everywhere. Not only does traditional Chinese civilization shape China's present and future in ways that influence our own lives, directly or indirectly. Not only has China been a high, complex civilization rooted in conditions and attitudes different from those with which Western civilization developed, so that it can serve us as a kind of distorting mirror in which, by seeing what we are not, we might understand ourselves and our civilization more maturely. Basically, traditional Chinese civilization fascinates outsiders because it is one of humankind's vastest treasuries of cultural achievements and social experience, and to be ignorant of it would greatly diminish our appreciation of the wondrous variety to be found in the historical life of man.

The Land and the People

The Land

Among modern nations, China is second only to the Soviet Union in land area. It encompasses 4,200,000 square miles and stretches continuously as far as from Maine to Cuba and from Boston to San Francisco. Much of this territory consists of frontier regions that are not densely populated by Chinese and came under China's political control only late in traditional times. They form buffer zones on the west and north that traditionally kept the Chinese heartland insulated against unwanted influences from other, distant centers of civilization in India-Pakistan, the Middle East, and Europe. From west to east, these frontier areas are:

1. Tibet, a barren plateau averaging 15,000 feet above sea level and surrounded by the most formidable mountain masses on earth.

2. Sinkiang, the "New Dominion" that Westerners used to call Chinese Turkestan, which is partly an oasis-studded desert choked at the western end by mountain passes of 20,000-foot elevation, and partly a bleak grassy plateau, or steppe, suitable only for nomadic grazing.

3. Inner Mongolia, beyond the Great Wall, stretching 1,500 miles east-west atop North China mountains, a region only marginally usable for agriculture, separated from the steppes of Outer Mongolia by a great gravel wasteland called the Gobi.

4. Manchuria, the fertile basin of the Liao River in the northeast, hotter in summer and colder in winter than the Chinese heartland and separated from it and Mongolia also by mountains.

The traditional Chinese heartland, commonly called China Proper, comprises the 18 provinces outlined on the map on pages x-xi, above. Its major natural division is between north and south, along the Ch'in-ling (Tsinling) mountains that stretch from the Tibetan foothills eastward toward the Pacific Ocean between the Yellow River drainage area to the north and the Yangtze River drainage area to the south. These two major regions are conventionally called North China and South China.

North China. North China includes a highland zone in the west (Kansu, Shensi, Shansi), a substantial lowland plain in the center (Hopei, Honan, and parts of Shantung, Anhwei, and Kiangsu), and in the farthest east the rocky Shantung promontory pointing toward Korea and Japan. In winter the whole area is swept by cold, dry air currents out of the deep interior of Eurasia; in summer it gets warmth but relatively little rainfall from air currents moving inland from the Pacific Ocean. North China is thus characteristically a brown, dusty place in which agriculture can prosper only by the use of irrigation water from the Yellow River and its tributaries. It is a land of huts with pounded-earth walls and thatch roofs; of broad roadways, carts, horses, donkeys, oxen, and even camels; of dry-field crops such as millet, wheat, and sorghum; of a toilsome life of struggle to overcome the difficulties and vagaries of nature.

The northwestern highlands are thickly covered with a fine-grained soil called loess, which has been deposited there for many centuries by the winds from Inner Asia. The Yellow River, originating in Tibet, cuts through the loess and picks up a heavy burden of silt, which it redeposits as alluvium across the lowland plain to the east. Fortunately for the Chinese, this redeposited loess is a highly productive soil when well watered. Unfortunately for the Chinese, on the other hand, the Yellow River deposits silt at such a rate that its bed is constantly rising. It must be diked ever higher, until the river flows above the rooftops of nearby villages. Inevitably the dikes break, and the river floods the plains for miles around. When it ultimately finds a new channel to the Pacific, the diking commences again. Again and again in China's long history the river has flooded so devastatingly that it has shifted its outlet to the sea back and forth from the north side of the Shantung promontory to the south. It is because of damage done and lives lost on such occasions that the Yellow River has been known as China's Sorrow.

South China. In the south nature is milder. Rainfall is abundant through a long warm summer; and the Yangtze River, which also originates in Tibet, flows through the fertile and temperate Szechwan basin in the west, cascades down mountain rapids onto the central plain, and then meanders harmlessly across a lush green region abounding in tributary streams and pleasant lakes. Amid the hills of the far south and southeast, small valleys line the coasts; and on the mountainous southwestern plateau of Yunnan, Kweichow, and Kwangsi provinces are great jungly forests, forming a natural barrier between the Chinese and the Thais and Burmese of mainland Southeast Asia.

South China yields flowers and fruits of every sort, and conditions are almost ideal for the cultivation of paddy (that is, flooded-field) rice. This staple crop of the south requires intensive, garden-scale cultivation but produces two and in some areas three harvests from one field every year. The whole of the south is so well watered that the water buffalo is the only draft animal of any use, houses must be built of stone or of wood and plaster and roofed with tile, and travel and transport by water, in small sampans and large junks, is the general rule everywhere. Land travel is restricted to narrow paths between flooded fields or over rugged hills, and overland transport is entrusted to coolie carriers. In many towns and cities, house-lined canals serve as streets, in Venetian fashion.

It should now be clear that, contrary to a common assumption among outsiders, China Proper despite its dense population is not a vast agricultural plain. Rather, it is a checkerboard of small to medium-size valleys and plains separated from each other by rugged terrain not suitable for agriculture. To be sure, the great North China Plain is one of the world's most extensive cultivated areas, but it is dwarfed by the corn and wheat belt of the American Midwest. Even in modern times, when the Chinese have made strenuous and imaginative efforts to expand agriculture so as to feed their enormous and ever growing population, they have never succeeded in bringing more than 20–25 percent of the land surface of China Proper under regular cultivation. Moreover,

the land is so fragmented into regions with distinct geographic characteristics that one question always arises early
in consideration of Chinese history: Why did China not
evolve into many separate nation-states in the European
style?

The People

China's geographic fragmentation is compensated for in
part by racial unity, that is, the similarity of physical
characteristics among its people. All Chinese are of the
Mongoloid ("yellow") racial stock, with virtually no hint of
Caucasoid (white) or Negroid (black) influence. Indeed, all
the peoples with whom the Chinese had significant contacts
until modern times were Mongoloid like themselves, with
relatively sallow complexions, straight black hair, and what
Westerners think of as slanting eyes.

Nonetheless, there are physical differences among the
Chinese. For example, North Chinese are generally taller and
more robust than South Chinese. Moreover, there are major
cultural differences. The majority of the population by far
consists of relatively "pure" Chinese by culture, who know
themselves as the Han people after the name of an admired
early dynasty. The many non-Han peoples who are also part
of the Chinese nation today principally include incompletely
assimilated Manchus in the northeast, still largely nomadic
Mongols in Inner Mongolia, Moslems in the western parts of
China Proper and in Sinkiang, Tibetans, and scores of
unassimilated, relatively primitive tribes in the hilly regions
of the south and southwest. These primitive tribesmen, or
"aborigines," who are related to the Vietnamese, the Thais,
and the Burmese of Southeast Asia, are descendants of the
earliest known inhabitants of South China. They were gradually ousted from the agricultural valleys and plains by the
Han Chinese expanding out of their original homeland on the
North China Plain. The most common collective name for
these aborigines is the Man, but they include many culturally

differentiated groups known as the Chuang, the Miao, the Lolo, the Moso, and so on.°

The Moslems differ from the Chinese proper in their religion and religion-oriented matters such as dietary laws. Other minorities differ from the Chinese principally in that their traditional languages are non-Chinese. From the point of view of language, as a matter of fact, modern China is a seriously divided nation. Not only do the non-Han minority peoples overwhelmingly not use Chinese as their mother tongue; even the Han peoples speak variants of Chinese that differ as substantially from each other as, for instance, the Romance or the Germanic languages do. The variations are considerably greater than those that mark the many dialects of English. A native speaker of Cantonese from the south simply cannot understand or make himself understood among speakers of Pekingese in the north. So great are the differences, and so numerous are the regional variations, that some linguists are inclined to consider Chinese not a language, but a family of languages comparable to the Romance and Germanic families in the hierarchy of the world's language groupings.

Most commonly, however, Chinese is considered to be one language comprising a large number of dialects and belonging to the language stock known as Sino-Tibetan. Chinese is clearly related to Tibetan, Burmese, Thai, and Vietnamese. There is no known linguistic relationship at all, however, between the Chinese and their various northern neighbors, with whom they have struggled throughout history. The northerners have spoken languages of the Turkic, Mongolian, and Tungusic (Manchu, etc.) families, which belong to an entirely different language stock called Altaic, as Korean and Japanese do also. Chinese is as different from all these

---

° In the following discussions, the word Chinese normally refers exclusively to the Han peoples, the developers and carriers of what we call traditional Chinese civilization.

languages as it is from English and the other Indo-European languages.

The Language and the Writing System

The form of the Chinese language that is spoken by the vast majority of Chinese nationals, the inhabitants of North China and of the Yangtze River drainage area, is known to Westerners as Mandarin and to the Chinese as *kuo-yü,* "the national speech." Its use as a standard speech form has been promoted by all modern Chinese governments for the sake of the easy nationwide communication considered essential for modernization. The major linguistic characteristics of Mandarin are as follows:

1. Single-syllable sounds are its basic semantic units, or morphemes. That is, Chinese words are monosyllabic sounds that we alphabetize or romanize in such forms as *ai, cheng, chü, fa, hsiao, huan, i, ko, liao, mo, nu, p'ei, sang, shih, ts'ang, wo,* and *yin.* The syllables are consistently open, that is, ending in vowels or in such sounds as -n or -ng. Only about 400 syllables are used in Mandarin, and in speech they are often combined in binomes or other multisyllabic sequences: for example, *chu-i* (two sounds that independently mean "master, principal" and "idea" combined to suggest principle or the suffix -ism) or *ch'eng-shih* ("walled town" and "marketplace" combined to mean city).

2. The morphemes or words are not inflected. There are no conjugations or declensions to indicate tense, mood, number, gender, and the like. Moreover, a word is used without any change of form as a noun, a verb, an adjective, an adverb, or any other part of speech. Thus *tsou* carries all the meanings go, to go, going, is going, goes, went, has gone, had gone, should have gone, etc. Tense, number, and other such things are often clear enough because of context and word order; and the Chinese can make their speech more specific when they wish by adding clarifying words or sounds, to produce a sentence, for example, that we might translate literally as

"You-all before go-finish, huh?," meaning "Have you (plural) gone?"

3. Homophones or syllables that otherwise sound alike can be differentiated by being pronounced in different tones. Four tones are used in Mandarin: a high level tone, a rising high tone, a falling and then rising tone, and a sharply falling tone (often suggested graphically as follows: ‾ ˊ ˅ ˎ). This tonal variation is what gives Mandarin the sing-song quality that Westerners commonly hear in it. By the use of tones the basic 400 monosyllabic sounds in the Mandarin vocabulary can theoretically become 1,600 tone-inflected sounds that seem distinctly different from each other to the Chinese ear.

4. Word order is generally similar to that of basic English: noun (subject) + verb + adjective + noun (object).

What has always intrigued Westerners most about Chinese is the way in which it is written. The Chinese have never spelled out their language in alphabetic letters. Rather, they write in nonalphabetic characters of three basic types, illustrated in the chart on the following page.

Learning to read and write such characters is of course not easy. Thus only a small proportion of Chinese have ever become literate. Modern Chinese governments have hoped to devise some scheme by which the writing system might be alphabetized successfully, but in vain. There are simply too many homophones; for example, there are 137 separate characters or words romanized as *i* among the 7,773 characters in the most popular Chinese-English student dictionary. The number of ways one might conceivably alphabetize the sound "ee" is very limited, even if one differentiates tones in some fashion, as with superscript numerals: i^1, i^2, i^3, i^4 (a common system).

The burden that the writing system puts on the Chinese, which is felt particularly as they strive for the universal literacy that is expected of modern nations, is offset in some degree by the advantages of the system. Characters far surpass any alphabetic letters in their intrinsic aesthetic

PICTOGRAPHIC FORMS

子 CHILD (from ancient form 孚)

木 TREE

女 WOMAN (from ancient form 𩇕, apparently suggesting a submissive, kneeling figure with arms clasped at the wrists)

IDEOGRAPHIC FORMS

Simple:

一 ONE   二 TWO   三 THREE   上 UP   下 DOWN

Compound:

好 GOOD (woman and child)   安 CONTENTMENT (woman under roof)

家 HOME (pig under roof)   明 BRIGHTNESS (sun and moon)

A TYPICAL LOGOGRAPHIC FORM

桐 T'UNG, a genus of tree, combining the meaning of 木, TREE (pronounced *mu*), with the sound of 同 T'UNG (meaning together)

The Chinese writing system

appeal, especially because of their pictorial and ideographic qualities, but even without taking these into account. The character 愛 simply is a more beautiful visual object than our spelling l-o-v-e; and a page of fine Chinese calligraphy is recognized everywhere as a piece of fine art. Moreover, the writing system is perfectly suited to the nature of the Chinese language, with its multitude of homophones and dialects. Chinese may not always understand what they say to one another, but if they are literate they can communicate in writing. Thus Chinese writing has been a powerful cohesive force in the evolution of Chinese civilization. Anything in writing has had universal currency among the literate throughout the whole of China, overcoming dialectal boundaries. In this regard Chinese characters are like the so-called Arabic numerals 1, 2, 3, etc., which are understood throughout the modern world, despite being spoken differently in different languages.

Because any Chinese character specifies what is meant more clearly than its monosyllabic pronunciation, written Chinese can be more concise than spoken Chinese. Until the twentieth century the Chinese thus wrote for the most part in styles divorced from speech, even in grammatical patterns. These written styles are collectively called *wen-yen* (the written word), whereas spoken Chinese is called *pai-hua* (plain speech). This century's greatest progress in spreading literacy in China has resulted from the abandonment of *wen-yen* and the adoption of *pai-hua* patterns for writing. Now the Chinese can at least understand writing when it is read aloud, which was not possible when the writing was in the formal *wen-yen* style.

Some Characteristic Social Patterns

The Chinese are very self-conscious about their uniqueness among the peoples of the world, and in modern times most Chinese have consciously striven to retain and strengthen those qualities that give them their unique Chineseness. They speak proudly of the Chinese "essence." There are many opinions about what this essence includes, but in any definition it is a special combination of many elements, certainly including the writing system and the vast corpus of national literature it carries, and the long historical heritage that is summarized in what follows. Among other elements that are commonly emphasized, two deserve introductory attention here: the intensely agrarian Chinese economy and the close-knit organization of Chinese society.

The Agrarian Economy

Since the time when the Chinese emerged from prehistory as a recognizable nation, their economic life has been dominated by sedentary farming work. Though in earliest times agriculture was heavily supplemented by hunting and herding, these activities steadily lost importance as the Chinese multiplied and brought new lands under cultivation. Fishing always remained a major supplemental activity in suitable areas, but animal husbandry eventually dwindled to the maintenance of such edible scavengers as pigs, chickens, ducks, and dogs. For at least the last 1,000 years, meat has been a great rarity in the diet of the average Chinese. Similarly, though commerce and craft industries developed in many ways and at times on a scale far surpassing that of the contemporaneous Western world, the need for basic food production to sustain China's population bred an ideology that always gave first priority to agriculture and sometimes actively discouraged commercial development. China became partly a nation of great bustling urban centers much earlier than Europe, but it nevertheless remained—and remains today—primarily a nation of peasants, with 80 percent or more of the population directly engaged in agriculture.

Chinese agriculture is one of the world's most productive systems per acre, at a staggering cost in labor input. The rural scene, therefore, is not characterized by vast farm tracts under single ownership and management such as dominate the American Midwest. Rather, Chinese farms have normally been aggregations of several small and scattered plots, in some regions totaling no more than two or three acres per family. Some form of collective management existed in ancient times, and manorial estates existed occasionally thereafter. It is not known just when fragmentation of the land into garden-size plots became the norm; but that pattern has prevailed through most of the past 2,000 years.

So as to have easy access to their small, scattered holdings, peasant families have clustered their dwellings in small villages ranging in size from a score or so households to hundreds, always within easy walking distance to the surrounding fields. Such villages lie within sight of one another across most of China's plains and valleys. Among them, small market towns have multiplied over the centuries, so densely that the most distant villager could walk to and fro in not more than a day. Here small shops and workshops provided for the villagers' regular marketing needs, teahouses offered them entertainment and opportunities to exchange news and stories, and large landowners or landlords made their homes. Some small towns also developed around mines, coastal or river landings, religious establishments, and strategically located military garrisons. Those that were advantageously situated became the natural wholesale marketing centers for larger regions or centers of governmental administration, and thus grew into large towns and cities as the population grew.

The original millet and wheat crops of North China have been supplemented by sorghum since the thirteenth century. Paddy rice has steadily spread from South China into all areas where the necessary flooding of fields has been possible. In addition to these basic cereal crops, Chinese agriculture normally produced vegetables and fruits of great variety. Farm households also engaged in the production of hemp and silk from earliest times, tea from about the second century A.D., cotton from the twelfth and thirteenth centuries, and in more recent times such supplemental produce as peanuts, maize, both sweet and Irish potatoes, and tobacco.

For the past 1,000 years or more, peasants have been part of a complex marketing operation of a kind that their European counterparts have known only for the past 200 years or so. Farmers were in close enough touch with the market towns and even the cities to be able to adapt themselves readily to fluctuating conditions in the urban markets. In normal times a rice farmer might devote himself solely to cultivating his rice, leaving his wife to earn extra family income by buying silkworms, feeding them carefully with mulberry leaves, and selling the coarse silk threads for further processing in town shops—or perhaps by spinning and weaving silk and cotton for urban entrepreneurs. In special market circumstances, however, the whole family might devote itself to producing the largest possible rice harvest to be sold entirely as a cash crop. In such ways there was a level of rural-urban interaction in late traditional China that we ordinarily do not associate with premodern societies; and a large number of Chinese peasants, perhaps the majority, were involved with urban life sufficiently to be thought of as suburbanites rather than as isolated, self-sufficient, ignorant country folk.

Traditional industrial production, in addition to textiles, principally included salt, ceramics, and metals. Iron came into general use not later than the fifth century B.C.— including cast iron, which was not to be known in Europe for another 1,000 years—and by the tenth century A.D. the Chinese were producing steel. At the same time the perfection of porcelain and the appearance of printed books added impressive new elements to the basically agrarian economy. It was not until the nineteenth century, however, that China, in response to the challenge of the modern West, conceived of and tried to begin industrializing on a national scale.

Social Togetherness

The Chinese do not value rugged individualism. From earliest times they have striven for tight social organization, and over time they developed great skill at organizing themselves. Although they have experienced repeated, often chaotic national upheavals, and perhaps for that very reason, they generally fear disorder (*luan*) as the greatest social calamity.

Individual Chinese have consequently been taught from infancy that they can survive and prosper only by belonging to groups, and that individuals who fail to serve and derive support from their groups will suffer miserable, pitiful lives, virtually as social outcasts. Thus when something has to be done, the Chinese are inclined to think of doing it in and through groups, not on their own.

The family. The principal group to which a Chinese traditionally belonged was the nuclear family, and this rather than the individual was considered the basic unit of society. The man was the unquestioned head of the family in the eyes of the community and the government, wielding almost total authority over his wife and children, answerable and responsible to the community and the government almost totally for the conduct of all family members, owner of all property acquired by anyone in the family, and recipient of all family income. Normally, the household head could punish his wife and children—even kill an unfaithful wife or a disobedient son—with no fear of community reproach or governmental inquiry. To the extent permitted by his resources, he could take secondary wives and concubines. With his wife's counsel he arranged the marriages of all his children, making alliances with other families to his own best advantage.

Chinese of the last imperial centuries considered it ideal for sons, after marriage, to remain and develop their own nuclear families within the father's household and for their sons to do likewise, so that as many generations as possible might live together in a large extended-family household. On the death of a father, his property was by law divided equally among his sons, who then established separate households that in time might house new extended families of several generations.

Beyond the extended family was the lineage or clan, linking all the families that were related through the male line and resided in one region. The lineage's function was to organize the member households for collective purposes—to maintain a temple, a school, and collectively owned property, the income from which could be used to help promising young men of the lineage get higher education; to give assistance to financially troubled member households; and to sponsor other programs that benefited the families and their individual members. Such lineages kept genealogical registers so that everyone knew his standing in the kin hierarchy, and the elders were expected to mediate family disputes. The strength of lineage organizations varied from locality to locality; they were especially strong and influential in the south in recent centuries.

The family and all its extensions were bound together in ancestor worship. In religion, a family was something like an indefinitely perpetuated corporation. The dead ancestors and the still unborn descendants were alike considered members, the living members being merely temporary trustees or custodians. The family temple contained tablets representing the spirits of the dead. The family head was expected to make regular offerings and reports to them, and hoped for their help in protecting the living family and furthering its interests.

Families were identified by surnames, which were universal in China well before the time of Christ. All persons of the same surname were considered descendants of a common ancestor, and persons of the same surname were forbidden to marry even if their nuclear families had lived in opposite corners of China for centuries and had no traceable blood relationships.

Sons owed absolute obedience to their parents, and especially their fathers. They secondarily owed allegiance to the extended family and, beyond that, to the lineage or clan. A son's most sacred duty was to marry and beget sons to carry on the family line. From a religious point of view this was essential for perpetuating the ancestral worship that sustained the dead and prevented their becoming "hungry ghosts" without living descendants to serve them. From a practical point of view having sons was essential to ensure one's own well-being in old age.

Since girls on marrying left their natural parents and

became members of their husbands' families, and since good marriages could be arranged for girls only if they took substantial dowries to their husbands, families were not joyful at the birth of daughters. In very poor families infant daughters were sometimes killed, especially in times of severe economic strain, and maturing daughters were commonly sold into prostitution or into bondage as servants or slaves in better-off households. The best hope any girl had was to marry respectably and then, as soon as possible, bear sons. She also had to do everything possible to win the favor of her husband's parents, and she usually became virtually a servant to her mother-in-law. If she displeased her husband's parents, and especially if she failed in good time to produce a child, her marriage could be nullified and she could be returned to her own parents in disgrace—unless her natural family was wealthy and influential enough to protect her from such treatment.

Non-kin groups. In addition to their families, traditional Chinese belonged to other kinds of groups that both helped them and made demands on them. One's local community, whether a rural village or an urban ward, was a relatively autonomous, self-regulating group that was expected to protect and discipline all its families and foster their general well-being. Individuals were also registered inhabitants of larger areas controlled by the lowest level of formal government, known as *hsien* (counties or districts); and shared cultural traits gave every Chinese a sense of comradeship with other natives of his province, a territory comparable in size and importance to an American state. Only in modern times were the Chinese forced to think of themselves seriously as being affiliated together in the national entity, China as a whole.

Beyond the realm of these natural affiliations based on kinship and residence, Chinese commonly developed important relationships in groups of many other sorts: craft and mercantile guilds, literary clubs, do-good associations of every kind, religious sects, and secret societies. In all these voluntary and involuntary ways the Chinese bound themselves together in networks of groups, to such a degree that everyone had innumerable "contacts"; and relying on such contacts was the normal way to get along safely and successfully in the world. The thought of having to cope alone with the vicissitudes of life was simply dreadful.

The sense of togetherness that grew out of all these group affiliations must have been stiflingly oppressive for many Chinese. But it also gave individuals the security of knowing precisely who they were and where they belonged. Moreover, the closeness of human relationships inevitably made for flexibility and tolerance. Since a person could not escape his social ties, he had to bear with aberrations in others that could not reasonably be changed. Fathers had to expect that their sons would occasionally be disrespectful, and sons had to expect that their fathers would occasionally be tyrannical; there was little to gain in making much ado about it in either case. China should therefore not be thought of as a nation of meek conformists. On balance, individual Chinese tend to be strong personalities. Even Chinese women, for all their formal submissiveness, as often as not can be quite intimidating when aroused. And though conformity to prevalent norms was indeed a social goal, Chinese history yields as marvelous a gallery of nonconformist eccentrics and rogues as the world has known.

Some Notable Patterns of Chinese History

Chinese history is very long, and there are many ways it can be divided into manageable segments. Western historians often take the broad periodization of Western history—antiquity, the Middle Ages, and modern times—and impose it on Chinese history arbitrarily, without realizing how inadequately it fits. Communist historians usually try to use Marx's notion that societies inevitably and inexorably evolve from slavery to feudalism to capitalism to socialism to fully classless communism; they suggest that though slavery early gave way to feudalism in China, foreign conquest and Western imperialism aborted the natural evolution to capitalism, so that the nation was feudal from antiquity to the establishment of the socialist People's Republic in 1949. Intellectual historians, art historians, literary historians, and other specialists might justifiably define the ages of Chinese development according to their own special interests. The ideal system of periodization would take into account as many as possible of all the elements that make up Chinese civilization—political, socioeconomic, intellectual, and cultural—and pinpoint those turning points in history when the interrelated aspects of Chinese life all experienced significant changes.

The Dynastic Cycle

The Chinese themselves have traditionally treated their history as a succession of dynasties, in each of which one family monopolized the throne. This reflects a belief that developed in China's antiquity and became a foundation stone of all subsequent political thought—that rulers of China, without themselves being divinities or enjoying a divine right to rule in the traditional Western sense, ruled in hereditary succession as earthly legates of Heaven. That is, rulers possessed a Mandate of Heaven (*t'ien-ming*) to rule. But no one could become ruler without Heaven's approval. Thus anyone who successfully challenged a ruler demonstrated by his success alone that Heaven no longer approved of his predecessor and had passed its mandate to him. So dynasties rose and fell, being considered legitimate and deserving of the people's allegiance only so long as they were able to maintain their de facto control of the country.

The idea of the Mandate of Heaven made it necessary for the Chinese to consider the founder of every dynasty a good man and the last ruler of every dynasty a weak or wicked man. The concept that dynasties had cyclical lives has a certain limited validity. In general, no one could overthrow his ruler and found a new dynasty without being a strong leader capable of rallying widespread support. And it was almost predictable that in time his descendants, reared in a palace secluded from the realities of the world, would be less capable, and that the dynastic government would sooner or later become less disciplined, less alert, and less successful in responding to changing situations, until general dissatisfaction made it possible for another strong leader to arise, topple the government, and start a new cycle.

Presenting Chinese history in dynastic cycles, however, is not very enlightening for modern students because there were numerous noteworthy dynasties of longer or shorter duration, and a change of dynasty did not necessarily correspond to significant change in any other aspect of Chinese life. Presenting Chinese history solely as a succession of dynasties is even duller and less meaningful than presenting American history as a succession of presidents.

Unity and Disunity

More significant than the succession of Chinese dynasties is the fact that China passed through cycles of political unity and disunity. Unifying China, with all its geographic and cultural diversity, has always been a major achievement, and keeping it stably unified has always been difficult. In its great ages of political unity China has invariably enjoyed material affluence, military strength, and the flowering of culture. At such times the Chinese have extended their influence over all East Asia; and nearby peoples such as the Vietnamese, the Koreans, and the Japanese have eagerly transformed their cultures by borrowing from them. When China collapsed into separate regional polities, its influence abroad necessarily waned, its domestic values came into question, and there was great social and cultural ferment, which eventually produced a new pattern of life in a new age of unity. The great ages of stable national unity, of which the Chinese are naturally most proud, and the turbulent ages of disunity and disorder are equally important in the study of China's historical development.

Southern Expansion

One of the clearest and most fundamental themes that emerge from the study of Chinese history overall is the gradual, relatively steady expansion of the Chinese people—that is, the so-called Han people—southward from their place of origin in North China, ultimately to fill up the China Proper of today. In this expansion the Chinese did not move into an uninhabited wilderness; nor did they displace wholly alien aborigines in a process akin to the westward movement in American history. When Chinese civilization arose along the Yellow River, the south was occupied by peoples related to the Chinese, both in race and in language, whose cultures were then not far below the Chinese level. The Chinese expansion southward was accomplished in part by the relatively peaceable assimilation of those neighbors who, individually or in groups, were attracted by the advantages of becoming Chinese, in part by the forcible subjugation and slower assimilation of those who challenged Chinese authority, and in part by the displacement of those who stubbornly resisted and withdrew before the advancing Chinese soldiers and settlers. The assimilation of the southerners is not complete even today, as is evidenced by the continuing existence of the non-Han minority peoples mentioned previously.

What is especially noteworthy about the expansion of China southward is that it was not a process of transplanting North Chinese and their original way of life unchanged in South China, or of transforming the original inhabitants of the south into North Chinese. Rather, it was a process by which new kinds of land, new peoples, and new cultural elements of all sorts were absorbed into China and Chinese culture, so that "Chineseness" was being transformed and redefined continuously. Colonization and migration played large parts in the process, to be sure; but the majority of modern Chinese living in the now densely populated south are less descendants of original North Chinese than descendants of original non-Han southerners. Similarly, the dominant peoples of Vietnam, Thailand, and Burma are in large part descendants of original non-Han peoples of South China who emigrated in historical times and mixed with the original residents of mainland Southeast Asia. Because of the widespread consequences of Chinese expansion, both domestically and abroad, each phase of that expansion was an important milestone of China's history.

Northern Invasions

Another major theme of Chinese history is the tension between the Chinese and their non-Chinese neighbors to the north, a confrontation between totally different cultures that was largely responsible for China's steady expansion southward. In the north the Chinese faced a succession of peoples who shared the Mongoloid racial characteristics of the Chinese but, as has been noted, were wholly unrelated by language—speakers of the Turkic, Mongolian, and Tungusic languages of the Altaic stock. Moreover, unlike the aborigines of the south, they had a nomadic, herding life-style that made them and the agrarian Chinese implacably hostile to one another.

In earliest times, when North China was forested and less parched than today, abounding in animals such as the rhinoceros that have not existed there for the past 2,000 years and more, the proto-Chinese were one of many neolithic peoples who hunted, herded, and did transient farming in the area. As the agrarian Chinese civilization emerged and flourished, and particularly as the North Chinese terrain and climate changed, those peoples who chose not to become Chinese increasingly committed themselves to nonagrarian ways. Cultural differences intensified, especially after the non-Chinese became horseback riders rather than chariot drivers and thus introduced full horse nomadism, probably in the ninth or eighth century B.C. Whether these earliest non-Chinese northerners were linguistic relatives of the Chinese or not is not at all clear. But by the third century B.C. Altaic-speaking horse nomads were in full command along China's northern frontier, and the hostility between Chinese and non-Chinese there that is so monumentally symbolized by the Great Wall had become an established pattern.

From the third century B.C. into the eighteenth century A.D. Chinese history in one sense was dominated by a long seesaw struggle to determine whether or not the Chinese could retain control of the North China Plain in the face of nomad challenges. When China was united and strong the Chinese not only defended their ancestral ground firmly, but pushed the nomads back, converting Inner Mongolia into a semi-agrarian appendage and exerting military and political influence in Outer Mongolia and Chinese Turkestan. When China weakened, nomad tribes and federations overran the Great Wall, raided and looted North China's towns and cities, and at times took control of the Yellow River region, sending Chinese governments and emigrants scurrying into the south for refuge. In the thirteenth century the Mongols of Chingis (Genghis) Khan, under his grandson Kubilai Khan, subjugated the whole of China Proper. After a century of humiliation the Chinese overthrew and drove out the Mongols, but in 1644 the Tungusic-speaking Manchus of the northeast brought China under alien rule again, in the last dynasty of the imperial age.

These cyclic interactions along the North China frontier had ethnic consequences similar to those that resulted from China's southward expansion. That is, though some North Chinese migrated southward to escape nomad harassments, others remained; and though some nomad invaders withdrew or were driven out after their raids and military occupations, others remained. Thus the population of North China did not retain the pure Han Chinese bloodlines and life-styles it may

once have had. It was regularly infused with new blood and
new cultural elements by the northern invaders.

These various themes will reappear often in the historical
summary that follows. In what seems to me far the most
justifiable and most enlightening periodization scheme, premodern China's evolution is dealt with here in three major
phases: an ancient formative age extending through the third
century B.C., an early imperial age covering the millennium
from 202 B.C. to A.D. 960, and a later imperial age fading out
in about 1850.

THE FORMATIVE AGE

Prehistory - 202 B.C.

By 202 B.C. China was already a very old nation with a complex and turbulent history. This long history can be divided into five phases as follows:

1. Prehistory.

2. The flourishing of a strong and cultured regional state in North China, called Shang.

3. The longest dynasty of China's history, Chou—a classical age in which the basic patterns of Chinese life and thought were established.

4. An era of incessant civil war in the last Chou centuries, when regional kings contended for control over the whole country.

5. A short-lived but important dynasty called Ch'in (whence comes the Western designation China), which brought China Proper under its military dominance and imposed a highly centralized, standardized national administration in a form of government we call imperial, but promptly collapsed so that China was plunged into civil war anew.

Prehistory

The Chinese are perhaps the only major people of world history who have no myths or legends about migrating from some other place of origin. They have resided in China forever, so far as can be determined; and they traditionally believed their history as a nation could be traced back to before 2500 B.C. Archaeology suggests, more realistically, that Chinese history properly begins about 1500 B.C. with the emergence of the Shang state.

In far older times, perhaps 500,000 years ago, parts of North China were roamed by one of earth's earliest hominid or humanlike creatures, Peking Man. His most important remains, including fragments of more than a dozen skulls, have been found in mountain caves southwest of Peking. Peking Man appears to have had a brain about halfway in size between the great ape and modern man, the ability to speak, and a hulking and stooped but erect posture. He knew fire and lived by hunting game and gathering wild tubers, berries, and other natural foods. Although he had some physical characteristics shared by modern Mongoloids, he cannot necessarily be considered their direct ancestor.

The rest of China's paleolithic, or Old Stone Age, development is not yet well understood. By about 12,000 years ago, however, China Proper was thinly occupied by a variety of Mongoloid peoples in neolithic, or New Stone Age, phases of development—living by a combination of hunting, animal husbandry, and primitive agriculture, making crude pottery, and residing in small village groups. Two of the widespread neolithic cultures that ultimately developed are especially noteworthy:

1. A painted pottery culture, which reached a peak about 3000 B.C. and was represented in many local varieties spread over the highland northwest of China Proper. This culture's hand-coiled pottery was of red, black, and gray clay and was normally decorated with whorls and curvilinear geometric patterns in red or black pigment.

2. A distinctive black pottery culture, which evolved somewhat more slowly in the eastern lowlands of North China, and then spread along the whole China coast from Manchuria almost to Vietnam. Inland, it spread everywhere except into the rugged southwestern mountains, even displacing the painted pottery culture in much of the northwestern loess highlands. This culture produced an undecorated, burnished black pottery made on the wheel. It developed in large walled villages built on river-valley

mounds and was supported by more varied agriculture and animal husbandry than its predecessors. It reached its peak of development about 2000 B.C., and the historical Shang state emerged out of one of its regional branches in modern Honan province.

Chinese writings of the first millennium B.C. refer to a pre-Shang Chinese dynasty or state called Hsia and to a succession of pre-Hsia culture heroes who introduced agriculture, trade, architecture, writing, and other ways of civilization. Of special interest among the pre-Hsia legendary rulers are Huang-ti (Yellow Emperor), who was thought to have reigned from 2697 B.C., to have introduced silk cloth, the bow and arrow, ceramics, and writing, and to have won a great victory over "barbarians" somewhere in modern Shansi province that established his leadership among the tribes of the Yellow River plain; Yao, who is credited with the development of the calendar, ritual, music, and a rudimentary central government; and Yao's chosen, unrelated successor, Shun, renowned as a filial son, in whose reign China was reportedly inundated by a great flood that led to the channeling of its great rivers for drainage. No archaeological evidence has been found to support these old written traditions, but Chinese scholars like to believe their national history actually begins with Huang-ti, and it seems entirely probable that archaeologists will one day be able to identify some neolithic group with the Hsia state of tradition. For the present, the archaeological and written evidence coincides only as regards the existence of the Shang state, and its dating is disputed. According to tradition, it was founded in 1766 B.C. and endured until 1122 B.C.

Shang

Of Shang political history we know very little. There was a succession of about 35 kings, some of whom inherited power as brothers rather than as sons. The royal domain was centered in a southwest-to-northeast arc in western Honan along the foothills that divide the highland from the lowland areas of North China. The capital was moved several times after its first establishment near modern Loyang; during the last three Shang centuries it was in the modern Honan region of Anyang, then called Yin (which came to be used interchangeably with Shang as the dynastic name). The state was often at war with surrounding non-Chinese—that is, non-Shang—"barbarians." The kings regularly conscripted 3,000 or 5,000 men, and on occasion even more, for campaigning, and their most powerful weapon was a compound bow, a type known to Westerners in more recent times as a Turkish bow—a powerful weapon indeed, commonly having a 160-pound pull. Finally, in about 1122 B.C., the last Shang king was defeated and overthrown by a satellite people to the west called Chou. In their hunting expeditions and military campaigns the Shang kings had extended their influence northward and eastward throughout the Yellow River plain and southeastward toward and perhaps into the Yangtze River valley. But their direct rule could not have extended far beyond the royal domain on a consistent basis.

Shang had some feudal characteristics. Areas beyond the royal domain were in the charge of personages whose titles were similar to those of feudal lords later, in Chou times. The common people were farming serfs or perhaps slaves; some ancient depictions show fieldworkers under the direction of whip-wielding overseers in scenes reminiscent of Egypt in antiquity. The royal government was staffed with men of hereditary status as nobles or aristocrats, but whether or not they enjoyed hereditary rights to positions or to fiefs is not clear.

Shang was a full-fledged civilization in that its capitals were genuine cities—large settlements with well-defined zones for religious and administrative functions, residences, and craft or service activities. Remains at Chengchow, no doubt the second Shang capital called Ao, give evidence of a city wall of pounded earth 30 feet high, from 65 to more than

100 feet wide, and over four and a half miles in circumference. The "great city Yin" at Anyang sprawled over at least sixteen square miles.

Especially notable in the Anyang area are the remains of 11 monumental royal tombs. Although not as monumental as the Egyptian pyramids, each is a pit some 30 feet underground measuring from 40 to 60 feet in diameter, with either two or four sloping access ramps up to 100 feet long. Many warriors and workmen were killed and placed in the tombs or along the ramps in "accompaniment burials" to serve the spirits of their dead masters—or perhaps to keep secret the tombs' locations. When considered together with the foundations of the large public buildings found at Anyang and the wall at Chengchow, such tombs testify that the Shang government was able to conscript large numbers of people for labor service as well as for military campaigning.

The Shang economy was predominantly agrarian; millet, wheat, and dry-field rice were the staples. Animal husbandry was of distinctly minor importance, and hunting seems to have been engaged in as much for military practice and sport as for supplementing the food supply. Shang had a standard decimal monetary system with cowrie shells as its basic unit, and archaeological remains include materials that must have come from as far away as southwestern China and even the South China Sea, so that Shang is assumed to have had far-reaching trading contacts. It is perhaps significant in this regard that the written character for Shang was later used to mean merchants.

Three culture elements especially distinguish Shang from prior stages of Chinese development:

1. Horse-drawn chariots. Horse remains have been unearthed from some pre-Shang settlements of the black pottery culture, but charioteering seems to have been a Shang innovation. The chariot was used both in hunting and in fighting. It could carry a bowman and a spearman as well as the driver, but whether in battle it was used somewhat like a

modern tank or primarily as a mobile platform from which commanders directed armies consisting of foot soldiers is not clear.

2. Fully developed bronze technology. Shang remains include a great variety of bronze tools and weapons, but the most notable finds are bronze ceremonial vessels of many shapes and sizes that are now scattered in museums the world over and are commonly considered the most magnificent bronzewares ever produced anywhere. They range in size up to 1,500-pound cauldrons, cast in clay molds in sections that were then fitted together with unsurpassed skill. They are commonly decorated in encircling bands with geometric designs. The most famous design is one called the *t'ao-t'ieh*—a highly stylized, unidentifiable animal figure dominated by two prominent eyes in a head seen frontally, with convoluted bodies extending winglike on both sides. The abstract character of the decor seems to link Shang bronzes aesthetically with the neolithic painted pottery culture, whereas the dominant forms link them structurally with the heritage of the black pottery culture.

3. Fully developed ideographic writing. The most dramatic discovery at Anyang, and one of the most important archaeological finds anywhere in this century, was a vast hoard of turtleshells and shoulderblades of cattle inscribed with the oldest known Chinese writings. These are so-called oracle bones, manipulated by professional, probably hereditary diviners on behalf of the Shang kings to communicate with the spirits of their ancestors. They reported notable royal activities and asked questions about what the kings could expect of the future—harvests, health, weather, births, hunts, military campaigns, and so on. Of about 100,000 such bones found in the buried royal archives, some 20,000 bear notations by the diviners giving their own names, the dates of divination, and the gist of reports that were made or questions that were asked. Equating the ancient characters with modern equivalents, one of the most difficult scholarly tasks

of modern times, has yielded much of what we know about Shang life, as well as the knowledge that the writing system itself had already reached full maturity, including all the pictographic, ideographic, and logographic types of characters that are illustrated in the Introduction. The inscriptions reveal that the spirits of the royal ancestors expected respectful service from the living and if favorably disposed could intercede on behalf of the living at the court of a supreme deity called Ti, or Shang-ti, who could not be approached directly in divination.

It was once thought that the apparently sudden appearance in China of sophisticated chariots, bronzes, and writing was evidence that the Shang ruling class had migrated into China, bringing these elements of civilization from somewhere afar across Central Asia. Subsequent discoveries of early Shang remains at Loyang and Chengchow, however, now show all these elements in developmental stages linked to the preceding neolithic cultures of North China. Although diffusion across Central Asia is by no means ruled out entirely, especially in the case of the chariot, it now seems probable that most if not all of the major characteristics of traditional Chinese civilization originated independently in China Proper. It seems increasingly possible, as a matter of fact, that a bronze-age, urban, literate civilization appeared earlier in China than anywhere else in the world.

The Chou Conquest

The Chou (sounds like Joe) peoples who overthrew Shang in about 1122 B.C. first appear in reliable accounts in mid-Shang times. They were then primitive frontiersmen of the western highlands. How closely they were related to the Shang peoples is debatable. It is probably not inappropriate to consider them "country cousins," peoples who spoke the same language as the Shang peoples but who had not fully shared in the development of Shang civilization and had absorbed some non-Shang cultural elements on the frontier.

Toughened but wearied by constant battling against the "barbarians" beyond them, the Chou peoples eventually settled in the Wei River basin of Shensi province, near modern Sian city. There they gradually learned the more civilized ways of Shang. Cultivating alliances with nearby tribes, and no doubt intermarrying with them as well as with the Shang peoples, they then began planning to take over the Shang domain. Their eventual success is attributed to three men whom later Chinese lavishly praised as "the sage-kings of old":

1. King Wen, or Wen Wang, a posthumous designation literally meaning Cultured King, who is credited with conceiving the grand plan of displacing Shang and with instituting the system of alliances that was later to make the plan work. Tradition also ascribes to him the nonmilitary qualities that became part of the Chinese conception of an ideal ruler: religious reverence, magnanimity, and great concern for the welfare of the common people.

2. King Wu, or Wu Wang (Martial King), King Wen's eldest son and successor. After at least one unsuccessful foray, he led an allied army eastward to defeat the Shang forces, and sacked the Shang capital at Yin in 1122 B.C. according to the traditional, but questionable, reckoning. The last Shang king set fire to his palace and died in its flames. King Wu installed a scion of the Shang royal family to serve as a subordinate ruler at Yin under the guidance of two Chou princes, and he himself withdrew to the Chou homeland in Shensi. He soon died, leaving the throne to a child in the established Chou pattern of strict father-to-son succession. Though King Wu was traditionally lauded as a stern and inspiring leader, he apparently had only limited ambition.

3. The Duke of Chou (Chou Kung), a brother of King Wu, who quickly assumed regental authority over the new king. This prompted the Chou princes at Yin, in collusion with Shang loyalists, to rise in rebellion; and for three years the Duke of Chou fought to quell the rebellion and bring the

eastern lowlands of North China under enduring Chou control. In the process he established what we know as a feudal empire, and he apparently invented, as a propaganda device, the doctrine of the Mandate of Heaven, already mentioned. Having totally destroyed the city of Yin, he built a new city at modern Loyang from which to oversee the unruly eastern peoples, and he relocated there what remained of the old Shang aristocracy. In his recorded harangues to these troublesome subjects he argued that Chou had not selfishly yearned to absorb Shang. Rather, he said, the Shang kings, after an excellent record in the beginning, had degenerated into tyrants, so that Heaven had been grossly offended by them and had commanded the reluctant Chou leaders to overthrow Shang in a punitive expedition.*

In one such harangue, the Duke of Chou made it clear that he himself was not only willing but even eager to accept the responsibility imposed by Heaven on Chou:

O, if you numerous officials cannot persuade yourselves to consider my commands sincere, you will then find that you cannot be obedient. All the people will say, "We will not obey"; you will become negligent and perverse, grossly violating the king's orders. Then your numerous regions will bring on themselves the wrath of Heaven, and I shall have to inflict Heaven's punishments, scattering you far from your lands. . . . It is now a new beginning for you. If you cannot be respectfully peaceable, then lay no blame on me!

The Duke of Chou also wisely understood that this undoubtedly new doctrine was a two-edged sword that could be turned against the Chou kings if they failed to live up to Heaven's expectations. He tirelessly lectured his royal nephew on the responsibilities and duties of a ruler, in terms that Confucius and his followers later adopted as the bases of

---

*Heaven (*t'ien*) was the Chou counterpart of the Shang supreme deity, Ti. Unlike Ti, Heaven was not an anthropomorphic god; but it was willful. After early Chou, the concept of Heaven predominated in Chinese thought. Later, in the nineteenth century, this aspect of Chinese history encouraged some Christians to suggest that the Chinese had indeed originally known God.

their political theories. After seven years as regent, the Duke of Chou turned the reins of government over to the maturing king, who is thought to have ruled effectively thereafter, earning his posthumous designation Ch'eng Wang (the Completing, or Fulfilling, King).

The Duke of Chou is the first credible great man of Chinese history, and traditional Chinese considered him a paragon of both civil and military virtues and the real consolidator of their civilization. Unless the early historical records are wholly misleading, this esteem is justifiable. Without his vision and determination, the Chou conquest might have ended as a mere looting raid, leaving Shang to recover and endure on the eastern plain of North China.

Chou Feudalism and Its Decline

The long Chou era is traditionally divided by historians into two parts: Western Chou, lasting from the dynastic founding in about 1122 B.C. to 771 B.C., when the royal capital was at Hao, near modern Sian in Shensi; and Eastern Chou, from 770 B.C. to 256 B.C., when the capital was at Loyang in Honan on the central North China plain. Two subperiods of Eastern Chou are commonly recognized: the Spring and Autumn (*Ch'un-ch'iu*) era from 722 to 481 B.C. and the Warring States (*Chan-kuo*) period extending from 403 actually beyond the termination of the royal dynasty to 221 B.C.

The Feudal Order

Feudalism in medieval Europe had many varieties, and the ancient Chou social and political order corresponds to none of them precisely. However, the Chou system had several characteristics that were widespread in European feudalism, such as the dominance of a hereditary warrior aristocracy, the sharing of political power between a king and an array of regional lords, and rituals symbolizing and presumably guaranteeing the allegiance of regional lords to the king. Reference to the Chou dynasty as China's feudal age is therefore common and, when properly understood, not inappropriate.

The Chou peoples and their allies came into the lowlands of North China as unwelcome intruders, and they established a military occupation. They did this by delegating royal kinsmen and allied chiefs, with their personal followers, to build walled garrison towns at strategic points in the newly subjugated territories, from which the surrounding populations were gradually pacified. In some instances existing local chieftains were permitted to retain their local powers if they were submissive collaborators. From the centers of regional power there spread clusters of satellite settlements given as fiefs to subordinates of the regional lords. Only in such a fashion could the Chou kings extend their royal authority from their domain in Shensi onto the eastern plain on a stable basis, and only in such a fashion could they appropriately reward the leaders who had aided in the overthrow of Shang.

In an age of primitive transportation and communications, the Chou empire was necessarily a loose-knit one. Consolidating the regional and local centers seems to have kept the ruling class occupied contentedly through most of the Western Chou era; and the kings extended national, central control over the regional lords as best they could. Royal armies, often personally assembled and commanded by the king, were scattered across the plain to defend the extended realm against threats from surrounding "barbarians" and to help regional lords pacify or eliminate the non-Chinese enclaves that continued to exist unassimilated among the Chou settlements even beyond the end of Western Chou. The whole realm was considered to be the king's property, and the regional lords were appointed by the king, though soon after the conquest the lords became hereditary in practice, and royal appointment became a formality confirming the accession of an heir. The kings also sent inspectors into the regional domains to ensure that royal policies were followed and, it seems probable, to see that supplies and equipment were sent to the royal armies according to a prescribed schedule of levies. There is no evidence of a national tax, however. The regional lords owed periodic gifts to the king, but these were no more than tokens of the lords' allegiance.

The ruling class, collectively called *shih* (warrior-officials), consisted of the original conquerors, submissive Shang aristocrats and local chieftains, and their descendants. Their sense of unity was strengthened by intermarriage, so that all considered themselves members of a vast dispersed family of which the king was head. Supported by their subjects, the shih devoted themselves to a non-laboring, increasingly cultured life, cultivating such elite arts as charioteering, archery, ritual, music, and literature. Artisans and traders were few; they resided in the garrison towns as retainers catering to the needs of the elite.

The common masses were serfs bound to the land on manorial estates from which the ruling class drew its revenues. In the late Chou centuries it was believed that Western Chou agriculture was organized in units of nine plots in a tick-tack-toe pattern, with each unit worked by eight families. The eight families separately cultivated the eight outer plots for their own sustenance but collectively cultivated the central plot, the produce of which belonged to the local lord. The families also resided in part of the central plot, where there was a common well. This arrangement was known to later theorists as a "well-field" system because the organizational pattern resembles the Chinese character meaning a well, and it was an ideal that appealed to land-tenure reformers through imperial times. But so neat a pattern is clearly an idealization and could never have existed in practice on an extensive scale.

The Growth of Regional States

For several centuries after the conquest the feudal system worked effectively enough so that the Chou kings were something more than figureheads. But as time passed the familial ties of the ruling class weakened, the regional lords developed local power bases, and in particular the lords on the periphery of the Chou realm expanded their territories, toughened their armies in wars with non-Chinese neighbors, and made their fiefs into large regional states, each as rich and powerful as the royal establishment.

The fragmentation of the Chou empire accelerated after 771 B.C. In that year the royal capital at Hao was raided and sacked by non-Chinese from northern Shensi, and the king was killed in the slaughter. After some confusion, one of his sons was installed as king the next year in the more central and less exposed city of Loyang under the patronage of a local lord. But the new royal domain was too small a base for the Eastern Chou kings to exercise more than nominal authority over the stronger regional lords. The old royal domain in Shensi was granted as a fief to a loyal noble and soon became one of the strongest frontier states, called Ch'in.

In the sixth century B.C. the Chou realm was thus a European-style group of nation-states in all but name. The central North China plain incorporated the royal domain and a score of other small and weak but cultured and prestigious domains, notably Sung governed by descendants of the Shang kings and Lu governed by descendants of the Duke of Chou. Encircling them were the large and powerful frontier states: Ch'in to the west and northwest in Shensi, Chin to the north in Shansi, Yen to the northeast in the Peking region of Hopei, Ch'i to the east in Shantung, and Ch'u to the south in the Yangtze River valley, which was still only partly Chinese in culture.

Because the Chou king no longer had any effective control over the large frontier states and because semi-barbarous Ch'u in the south was a recurrent menace to the small central states, the state of Ch'i was prevailed on in 681 to convene a conference of northern rulers to discuss mutual-defense arrangements. The conference resulted in a formal coalition, or alliance by treaty, sanctified by appropriate sacrifices and oaths, under the leadership of Duke Huan of Ch'i. The arrangement was approved by the king, and three years later, after further conferences involving more states, Duke Huan was formally granted the designation hegemon (*pa*). His responsibility was to preserve peace and the honor of the Chou king. The coalition was so successful that in 656 Ch'u signed a peace treaty and for the first time accepted formal vassalage in the Chou feudal order.

The institution of hegemon was a new one in Chinese history. Later Chinese made it a symbol of illegitimate and improper domination by force, the antithesis of a true king (*wang*), defined as a person who was entitled to rule by his birth and virtue. But a succession of hegemons from various states served China reasonably well during the Spring and Autumn era. They artfully supervised interstate diplomacy, convened interstate conferences at which grievances were aired and resolved, and kept the Chou empire intact. Nevertheless, the great regional states increasingly flexed their muscles at each other, and all-out civil war became ever more likely. Meanwhile, the sense of Chinese cultural unity grew weaker, as regional differences in language, in customs, and even in the forms in which characters were written became prevalent.

Early Chou Culture

The Chou kings practiced ancestor worship with ritualistic fervor and carried on the Shang tradition of casting elegant bronze ceremonial vessels. Some of the most magnificent early Chou bronze vessels were cast to commemorate the enfeoffment of feudal lords or notable service rendered to the king. In the interior bottoms of such vessels are often found inscriptions of long commendatory decrees, texts of greater length than any found in Shang bronzes. The factual details and the literary styles of these inscriptions have enabled modern scholars to evaluate the authenticity and reliability of traditional writings ascribed to the age. The outstanding Shang skills in bronze casting were lost after several Chou generations, however. The middle Chou bronzes are characteristically cruder in technique and are often over-adorned with vulgar animalistic attachments that distract from whatever rough appeal the vessels themselves may have. Then, in the late Chou years, there was a renaissance of the earlier stylistic elegance in bronzes. Some of the later bronzes, especially those associated with the southern state of Ch'u, are marvelously inlaid with gold, silver, or jade—flamboyant, but elegantly so.

Local varieties of pottery were meanwhile produced by craftsmen everywhere, and gold and silver were worked into luxury wares for the elite. Jade, some imported from Central Asia, was particularly treasured for its cool velvet-smooth feel and was used extensively for religious talismans. Jade carving was becoming a fine art, which it remained through subsequent Chinese history.

As in Shang times, writing was done principally with a brush and ink on bolts of silk and thin vertical slats of wood, usually bamboo. Because of the perishability of these materials, the only surviving writings from this period are the inscriptions in bronze vessels and a few on stone; no original brush writings of the Chou era are known today. Texts were transmitted by copyists over the centuries. All such writings attributed to Chou times are therefore of questionable authenticity and must be used with care. But a corpus of Chou literature has survived and has been enormously influential in the shaping of China's cultural tradition. This is especially true of five works that are universally known as the Chinese Classics:

1. The *Classic of Changes* (*I-ching*). This originated as a cryptic handbook for diviners but late in the Chou era, or perhaps even thereafter, it began acquiring commentaries

that lent it profound significance as a mystical revelation of the ever-changing cosmos. The basis of the work is a series of 64 figures called hexagrams, which exhaust all the possible sets of six combinations of unbroken and broken lines, for instance:

To each such figure was appended a brief, often seemingly nonsensical group of words. The text and its later commentaries were considered a source of wisdom and guidance by all levels of society in imperial times.

2. The *Classic of Writings* (*Shu-ching*). This is a disjointed collection of documentary pieces that are supposed to date from the legendary rulers Yao and Shun down through the first three Chou centuries. The early Chou materials, which make up more than half the bulk of the work, are generally considered genuine. Among these are several exhortations by the Duke of Chou, from one of which the passage on page 33 above is taken.

3. The *Classic of Songs* (*Shih-ching*). This is an anthology of stately ceremonial hymns and undoubtedly edited folk songs from the early Chou centuries. They are predominantly in monotonous lines of four beats—that is, four syllables or words. The work is considered the greatest literary monument of the formative age. One famous example of its folk songs is this two-stanza lament:

My Lord Is on Army Duty

My lord is on army duty.
There's no knowing for how long.
When will he come?

The chickens have nested in their crannies;
It's the end of the day.
The cows and sheep have come in.
But my lord is on army duty.
How can I not worry about him?

My lord is on army duty,
Not for a day or a month.
When shall we be together?
The chickens have roosted on their perches;
It's the end of the day.
The cows and sheep have come in.
But my lord is on army duty.
If only he doesn't hunger and thirst!

4. The *Spring and Autumn Annals* (*Ch'un-ch'iu*). This is a chronicle of events from 722 to 481 B.C. compiled in the small central state of Lu, and from its point of view, but reporting important events throughout the Chou realm. Its entries are identified by year, month, and day, but all are as terse as modern newspaper headlines, for example: "Marquis I-wu of Chin died." The text early acquired three commentaries, the most useful and famous being the *Commentary of Tso* (*Tso-chuan*) by an unidentifiable author. It apparently originated as an entirely separate narrative history; it gives detailed, lively accounts of most of the incidents that are headlined in the *Annals* and some that are not. It is generally considered an early masterpiece of narrative prose.

5. The *Classic of Rituals* (*Li-ching*). There is no such work, and probably never was one. This is a category consisting of three separate works: (a) the *Chou Rituals* (*Chou-li*), which despite its name purports to give a description of and prescription for government in the earliest Chou times; (b) the *Propriety and Ritual* (*I-li*), supposedly a prescription for proper conduct among the early Chou ruling class; and (c) the *Ritual Records* (*Li-chi*), a hodgepodge of tracts, including prescriptions for the conduct of funerals, mourning, weddings, banquets, and so on. The *Chou Rituals* and the

Propriety and Ritual were traditionally thought to have been written by the Duke of Chou, but all three texts are unreliable idealizations dating from late Chou times or later.

The Hundred Schools of Thought

The Chinese way of life that was developing in the Chou dynasty included distinctive patterns of thought appearing in such ancient works as the *Classic of Songs* and the *Classic of Writings*. There was very little interest in abstract philosophy. The emphasis was on ethics and politics, and this emphasis intensified as social and political disruptions increasingly undermined the old feudal order in the later Chou centuries.

Basic Religious Concepts

Common to most of the thinkers who emerged by the end of the Chou dynasty—and presumably common to the ancient Chinese people at large—was a view of the universe and of human life that differs significantly from the Western heritage. It is noteworthy, for example, that the Chinese felt no need to explain how the cosmos originated until long after Chou times. The world was taken for granted.

The Chou Heaven was not an awe-inspiring god, but simply a governing force that played a role in the universe akin to that of an earthly lord. Man had no "spark of the divine fire" that gave him an ennobling relationship with Heaven. But man did have a soul—two souls, in fact, a "physical soul" that on death went to Earth (which itself was spoken of as an impersonal deity in the same terms as Heaven) and a "spiritual soul" that on death went to Heaven. The Chinese Heaven was something like the essence of spirituality or abstractness, Earth was the essence of physicality or concreteness, and man was the living creature in which these essences blended in their most important form.

In addition, the universe was thought to house spirits of many kinds. Among these the spirits of one's own ancestors were of principal importance, for they watched over human affairs most closely and were to be respected, served, made proud, and not dishonored. There were also spirits or deities thought to inhabit mountains, rivers, unusual rock formations, and other impressive parts of the worldly scene. Some spirits were benevolent, but others were at least potentially hostile—just as, among the living, one could expect help from one's kin and fellow villagers but had to be prepared for possible harm from strangers.

It is especially worth noting that in the Chinese conception there was no great gap between the living and the dead or between the "real" world and the unseen universe. The cosmos was conceived of as a unity. To be sure, it contained a material part and an immaterial part, but it lacked the distinctions that we in the West make between everyday reality and the awesome unseen realm. To the Chinese, spirits and ghosts were revered or feared not because of what they were, but because of what they were capable of doing. It was only common sense to propitiate those spiritual forces that could protect and befriend one and to appease, deceive, bargain with, and outwit those that could cause trouble, as best one could. In other words, the Chinese understood full well that Heaven and the spirits could be offended, but they had no feeling that they might be sinned against.

Associated with the concept of Heaven in traditional Chinese thought from early times was the word *tao,* which originally meant a path or a way. In a cosmic sense, it became the Way in which Heaven functions or in which Heaven wills things to go. Ethically, Chinese spoke of the way of a ruler, the way of a minister, the way of a father, the way of a son, and so on, meaning whatever was thought to be proper conduct in accordance with one's place and duty.

Late in the Chou era cosmologists began suggesting that the Way of Heaven was implemented by two abstract motive forces called *yang* and *yin.* Yang was thought represented by the unbroken line of the *I-ching,* yin by the broken line. Yang and yin were associated, respectively, with strength and weakness, light and dark, male and female. Yang and yin were opposites but complementary and inseparable rather than antagonistic, and they were in constant pendulum-like inter-action. Their contrapuntal waxing and waning was thought to account for the creation of all particular things and the movement of the universe from day to night and through all its other phases, endlessly.

As the Chou order crumbled and political conditions brought chaotic civil war ever closer, a ferment of intellec-tual activity developed. For the most part, thinkers were absorbed with how states or individuals could make the best of the bad and steadily worsening conditions they faced, though the spectrum of late Chou thought was broad enough to include a series of abstract logicians. At the other extreme, intensely practical, were military theorists such as Sun-tzu (Master Sun) of the fourth century B.C., author of an as-tonishingly sophisticated work on strategy and tactics, *The Art of War (Ping-fa)*, which is still studied in military academies around the world. Between these extremes were advocates of highly varied doctrines. Masters had disciples, and schools of thought transmitted teachings from generation to generation in such abundance that the Chinese tradi-tionally called them "the hundred schools." Among them, three were to have the most enduring impact: Confucianism, Taoism, and Legalism.

Confucianism

Confucianism, like Christianity, changed markedly from age to age and at many times had competing, contradictory interpreters. It is consequently not easy to define Confucian-ism adequately for the whole of its history. But its fundamen-tal outlook stems from three thinkers of late Chou times— primarily Confucius himself and secondarily his followers Mencius and Hsün-tzu.

Confucius (551–479 B.C.), known to the Chinese as K'ung-tzu (Master K'ung), was apparently China's first independent, tuition-taking teacher. A native of the small central state of Lu, he sought in vain for a ministerial post in some state where he might put his teachings into practice. He died thinking himself a failure, but he left a group of disciples who passed along his teachings, which were soon collected in bits and pieces into a short work called the *Analects (Lun-yü)*. From its unsystematic jumble of the master's memorable sayings, we learn that Confucius was a great admirer of the Duke of Chou, conservatively believed that all would be well if only people would do what they ought to do, according to their social roles and their consciences, stressed the effectiveness of rule by moral example instead of by force, and humbly denied being anything more than an uninspired but dedicated teacher of the honorable ways of antiquity. He issued no threats and promised no certain rewards but exuded confidence that human beings, if they sincerely tried, could learn to live gratifying lives in an orderly, harmonious society.

Mencius (c. 372–c. 289 B.C.), or Meng-tzu, was much more arrogant, argumentative, and influential than Confucius. He was no doubt the most erudite man of his day, and he lived handsomely, with a host of disciples, off one feudal lord after another, dazzling them with his denunciations of their inadequacies. He expanded Confucius's doctrine of rule by example and brilliantly argued that individual ability was more important than status and pedigree. His most famous contribution to Confucianism is the idea that all men are equally born with the seeds of virtue in them, and that every man can fulfill himself—that is, can become a sage—by earnest cultivation of his instinctive goodness. His teachings survive in a memoir-like book of anecdotes, called simply the *Meng-tzu*.

Hsün-tzu (c. 300–c. 235 B.C.) saw the Chou dynasty fall in endemic civil war, and perhaps for that reason was a less optimistic interpreter of Confucius than Mencius. He was a tough-minded student of mankind and the world, and he wrote a well-reasoned series of essays on problems and how they might be solved; his book is known as the *Hsün-tzu*. He stressed the selfish qualities that all men are equally born with, and argued that man could indeed make himself good, as Mencius said, but only by disciplined study of the precepts and precedents of antiquity under an authoritarian teacher. His thinking was strikingly rational and unsentimental.

Collectively, these early Confucians left a heritage of esteem for the Establishment, as we might put it, and for the earnest, conscientious, rational search for ways to revive it and make it work for human happiness and welfare. None of the three was an intensely religious man in the normal sense.

Taoism

Early Taoism, which is the complementary opposite of Confucianism in a yang-yin sense, is represented by two intriguing, often mystifying books, the *Lao-tzu* (also called the *Tao-te-ching, The Classic of the Way and of Virtue*) and the *Chuang-tzu*. Almost nothing is known of the reputed authors, Lao-tzu and Chuang-tzu. Their basic reaction to the chaos of late Chou times was individualistic escapism as opposed to Confucianism's concerned reformism.

Taoist escapism derives from the view that the Way (tao) of the cosmos is a rather mechanistic operation that animates all things, makes them what they are, and makes no value judgments concerning them. Appropriate conduct for man, in consequence, is simply to be himself naturally and spontaneously and not to strive to change either himself or anything else; only then can he be in proper harmony with the cosmos. It not only follows that Confucian reformism disrupts the functioning of the cosmos and society; in the Taoist view, government itself is anathema because it inevitably suppresses individual spontaneity and should be ignored, destroyed, or if all else fails, used ruthlessly (in the way that the tao, or nature, is ruthless, as in a typhoon or earthquake) to keep the people in a state of primitive innocence and ignorance.

Taoism abounds in contradictions and puzzles, and of course it serves as a poor basis on which to build a stable society or state. It has nevertheless had great and enduring appeal for the Chinese, who have found in it consolation for their human weaknesses and worldly failures. Most traditional Chinese were Confucian and Taoist at the same time, and the blend is often credited for the flexibility and resilience that have allowed China to survive the trials of its long history.

Legalism

Legalism was not a school of thought in the Confucian or even Taoist sense. Rather, it was an attitude accumulated in administrative experience and expressed in a few writings about administration, focusing on efficiency in promoting both the state's interests and one's own interests in serving the state.

Legalism is primarily associated with the western state of Ch'in, which by following Legalist principles eventually overpowered its rivals and united China. One of the classic Legalist texts is the *Book of Lord Shang (Shang-chün shu)*, attributed to a chief counselor of Ch'in in the fourth century B.C. who laid the organizational foundation for Ch'in's later successes. The major Legalist synthesis is the *Han Fei Tzu*, written by an adviser to the Ch'in ruler who united China; and the most famous Legalist practitioner was the chief counselor of the short-lived Ch'in dynasty, Li Ssu. Both Han Fei Tzu and Li Ssu had once been students of the Confucian Hsün-tzu, whose authoritarian inclinations they developed into a single-minded emphasis on enriching and strengthening the state.

There are three noteworthy emphases in Legalist theory. The first is authority. Nothing can be accomplished unless one is in a position of authority. Therefore, always knowing where authority resides and carefully safeguarding one's authority, either as ruler or as minister, is of cardinal importance. The second is technique. The ruler must know how to manipulate his officials, and the minister must know how to manipulate his ruler. Otherwise, the ruler allows others to encroach on his authority, and the minister fails to make effective use of whatever authority is properly his. Finally, there is law. The Legalists thought that the state would survive and prosper only if people were made to do what was best for the state, by the appropriate distribution of rewards and punishments. Such a situation could be achieved, they believed, only if laws covered every possible contingency, were universally known, and were enforced so uniformly and promptly as to seem automatic, and in such exaggerated forms as to be maximally encouraging or discouraging.

In modern terms the Legalists were efficiency experts who believed that everyone, including the ruler, could and should be programmed computer-style so that the state would prosper and endure endlessly, whatever conditions might be encountered, regardless of what might be thought moral or immoral. Their vision far exceeded their abilities; and, as history was to show, their value system was not in tune with the developing Chinese national character.

The Warring States Era

The history of the last Chou centuries is dominated by one thing: the steady intensification of war. In the Spring and Autumn Era wars between feudal lords had been, at least in part, something like knightly jousts between teams of gentlemen. Honor and "face" were at stake, but often little else. In the fifth century B.C., however, attitudes began to change, and thereafter interstate wars became increasingly common and serious, and their consequences more devastating. Losers were stripped of their lands and commonly lost their lives; it was conquer or be conquered, kill or be killed, no holds

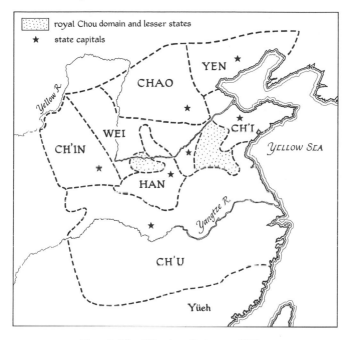

Map 1. The Warring States, c. 300 B.C.

barred. Ultimately, in the 200's, a time came when only three
powerful frontier states—Ch'in, Ch'i, and Ch'u, all now
greatly enlarged—were left to struggle for supremacy, with
constantly shifting boundaries.

Wars partly caused and partly resulted from great social,
economic, and technological developments. In the seventh
century B.C. large-scale water control and irrigation projects
had been undertaken in some states, and thereafter they
multiplied. Soon fertilization, field rotation, and the use of
animal-drawn plows were introduced. In consequence, agricultural production boomed, the population grew, larger and
larger armies could be put in the field and supplied, trade and
industry flourished, and there was rapid urbanization. In the
fifth century B.C. iron came into use for both tools and

weapons, making possible still greater intensification of agriculture and war. In the same century the old compound bow was supplemented with the crossbow, a more accurate new weapon equipped with a trigger mechanism. Iron spearheads, iron arrowheads, and triggered crossbows added greatly to the deadliness of war. Still another refinement came late in the fourth century B.C., when some northern states, confronted by the slowly developed horse nomadism of the non-Chinese on the steppes, converted infantrymen into cavalrymen. Soon all Chinese states had light cavalry to support their infantry forces, which had grown into massive regional armies as populations increased.

These changes completely undermined the traditional social order. The charioteering aristocrat early lost his dominant role on the battlefield when it became clear that his powerful ancestral spirits afforded him no protection or advantage against infantry masses and cavalry, and the religious foundation of the social hierarchy was seriously eroded. As war intensified, a person's pedigree counted for less and less. What counted was ability. Influential clan leaders began overthrowing weak lords or assuming regental power over them. Then commoners who excelled in agriculture or trade or fighting won recognition and rewards, and movement up and down the social scale quickened. Money came into widespread use, produced in various forms of coins cast in bronze and then copper. Before the end of the Chou era, what remained the standard monetary unit through the rest of traditional history had appeared—the *cash*, a round copper coin with a square hole in the middle so that coins could be strung on cords. A string of 1,000 *cash* became the normal market equivalent of a bushel of grain.

The opening and leveling of society in Warring States times can be attributed in large part to three considerations that figured heavily in the minds of regional rulers in their struggle to survive: the need for ever stronger armies; the need for ever greater economic production; and the need for the best managerial skills they could get. They had no choice but to set aside the social distinctions, the arbitrary discriminations, and the gentlemanly ways of the old feudal order. Lords competed with one another to improve the lot of the common people so that they would fight more zealously as soldiers and work more productively as farmers, and so migrants might be lured from neighboring states to swell the fighting and farming ranks. New ideas were accepted, if not always welcomed, in the hope that they might directly or indirectly help to strengthen and enrich the state; and wandering intellectuals peddled their panaceas everywhere, however practical or impractical. Rulers listened, not only in the hope of enlisting useful talents, but also in the fear that what they themselves considered crackpot notions might be implemented and found useful by enemy rulers.

The political history of this era is confusing in the extreme and of little intrinsic importance. There were short-lived alliances, large-scale betrayals, monumental massacres, diplomatic jugglings, famous acts of heroic dedication, and infamous instances of barbaric deceit and cruelty. The royal Chou domain disappeared in 256, and the royal line died out in 249 B.C., after long being ignored by all. The rush of events culminated in a series of military triumphs in the 230's and 220's by the state of Ch'in, from its base in Shensi. Ch'u fell in 221 B.C., and when the Ch'in armies then turned northward, Ch'i surrendered without a fight, and all China was united.

Ch'in

The Ch'in dynasty lasted only from 221 to 206 B.C. But its achievements were extraordinary and extraordinarily influential in China's subsequent development. Its history is dominated by two impressive figures. One was King Cheng, who came to the throne of his western frontier state in 247, led Ch'in through its campaigns of conquest, and ruled a united China till his death in 210 B.C. The other was the aforementioned Li Ssu, originally a subject of Ch'u, who became an adviser to King Cheng in 237 and later, as chief counselor, or prime minister, was the principal architect of the Legalist governmental system that Ch'in imposed on all China.

Centralization and Standardization

Ch'in's most notable achievement as a national dynasty was defeudalization—that is, obliterating those remnants of the Chou order that weakened centralized government, bred regionalism in politics and culture, and sustained hereditary social distinctions. Instead of parceling China into new regional fiefs, Ch'in divided it into 36 commanderies governed by nonhereditary appointees who were responsible to the central government for supervising subdivisions called districts or counties. All feudal land-tenure relationships were abolished; land became private property that could be freely bought and sold. A national tax was imposed in the form of a share of each farmer's principal crop. The old aristocratic class was deprived of its privileged status, and all Chinese became subjects treated by the government without discrimination according to a detailed, uniform law code.

The centralizing and equalizing processes were accompanied by standardization, most notably, of weights and measures, coinage, the axle widths of vehicles—and thought. Philosophical disputation was forbidden, praise of the past and criticism of the present were prohibited, and books other than the official Ch'in historical chronicle and certain kinds of utilitarian tracts were confiscated and burned. In 212 B.C. 460 offending scholars were executed and buried in a common grave as a warning against further defiance of the new thought-control laws.

Construction and Expansion

Ch'in's laws were so rigid and numerous that many thousands of Chinese quickly became convicts, assigned to labor on great construction projects that were also among the dynasty's notable achievements. The most famous of these was the first version of the Great Wall, which Ch'in created by consolidating the regional walls previously built by northern states for defense against non-Chinese nomads of Mongolia. According to legend, 1,000,000 laborers died in this work, and their corpses were thrown into the rubble that formed the core of the wall. Other great construction projects included highways, canals, irrigation systems, and a magnificent new palace at modern Sian, which had now become the imperial capital.

Ch'in not only conquered but expanded the Chinese world. The Yangtze River valley had already been largely assimilated in the late Chou centuries. Ch'in sent its armies farther south and established garrisons on the south coast that maintained at least nominal control over the aboriginal peoples as far south as Hanoi in modern Vietnam. Ch'in also campaigned northward into Inner Mongolia but did not subjugate territories beyond the Great Wall. In sum, Ch'in expanded its military and political control almost to the limits of modern China Proper. Its control over newly subjugated areas was so superficial, however, that the local inhabitants were by no means assimilated into the mainstream of Chinese culture.

Ch'in's Fate

When King Cheng overcame his principal opponents, he decided that the old title king was no longer adequate, having been usurped by regional lords for centuries. Combining two words of prestigious religious connotations, he created for himself the new title *huang-ti*, which we translate as emperor. On the assumption that his new Legalist governmental system would perpetuate itself forever, he decreed himself First Emperor, and his son eventually bore the prearranged designation Second-generation Emperor. But the Ch'in empire proved to be far from indestructible. Once the First Emperor's leadership was lost, the court was disrupted by

bickering grandees, and the countryside spawned bands of
dissidents who suffered from Ch'in's harsh laws. The vaunted
Legalist governmental machine failed to respond effectively,
and very quickly the Ch'in empire teemed with rebels. In 206
B.C. the capital at Sian fell, and for the next four years rival
contenders strove to unite China again. The First Emperor is
consequently known to history, ironically, only as First
Emperor of Ch'in.

Ch'in has fared badly at the hands of later Chinese
historians because of its harsh laws and cruel punishments,
the grandiose and often eccentric deportment of the First
Emperor, the anti-intellectualism of the regime and especially its anti-Confucianism, and the short life and rapid
collapse of the dynasty. But Ch'in had fully destroyed the
ancient feudal order and had demonstrated that China could
indeed be united, centralized, and strong with a new kind of
society and government. The establishment of this precedent
makes the short Ch'in era one of the major watersheds of
Chinese history.

THE EARLY EMPIRE
202 B.C. - A.D. 960

The civil war that brought Ch'in down was quickly resolved, and China began another millennium-long cycle from unity to fragmentation to new unity, from grandeur to institutional and cultural ferment to new grandeur. The era can be subdivided into three major periods:

1. Han, a dynasty lasting four centuries that was the East Asian counterpart of and contemporary with Rome in its golden age, under whose aegis China officially became a Confucian state, prospered domestically, and extended its political and cultural influence over Vietnam, Central Asia, Mongolia, and Korea before finally collapsing under a mixture of domestic and external pressures.

2. An era of division and confusion lasting almost another four centuries, during which the Han tradition withered in the south, non-Chinese invaders occupied the North China homeland, and Buddhism, imported from India, became the liveliest intellectual and cultural force in all parts of China.

3. Sui and T'ang, successive northern dynasties that reunited China, again established Chinese dominance over all East Asia now including Japan, and presided over the most renowned epoch of Chinese cosmopolitanism and cultural flowering, until a new round of domestic upheavals once again, in the tenth century, plunged China into warlordism and fragmentation.

The whole of this long era can be considered an aristocratic age in which wealth and political influence were monopolized by a relatively small class of great families, and military power counted for more than moral and intellectual caliber.

But there were impressive steps taken in the direction of a bureaucratic state system administered by men appointed because of their moral and intellectual merit as defined by Confucianism. Another important theme of the era's history is the introduction, the spread and development, and the religious primacy in T'ang times of Confucianism's greatest traditional challenger, Buddhism.

Former Han

The Han dynasty ruled a united China from 202 B.C. until A.D. 220, and its esteem among later Chinese accounts for their using the term "the Han people" to differentiate themselves from all other peoples who remained not wholly assimilated into the Chinese cultural mainstream. The Han ruling line was briefly interrupted by the usurpation of a famous reformer, Wang Mang, whose interlude on the throne from A.D. 9 to 23 is known as the Hsin dynasty. Historians therefore subdivide the Han period into two parts, Former Han, lasting from 202 B.C. to A.D. 9, and Later Han, from A.D. 25 to 220.

The New Consolidation

When rebels arose against Ch'in, they quickly revived the pre-Ch'in pattern of regional lords with feudal titles, giving allegiance to a new king of Ch'u. The alliance was unstable from the start, and struggles among the regional rebel chiefs gradually brought to the forefront a man named Liu Pang, whose power base was known as the Han fief. A coalition under his leadership established its national control in 202 B.C. His posthumous temple designation, by which he is best known to historians, was Han Kao-tsu.

Kao-tsu (Exalted Progenitor) was the first commoner to rule China, and he won the empire largely because of his troop discipline and the magnanimity with which he treated the people at large. He had no governmental program except to relieve the people of Ch'in's oppression. A coarse peasant

fighter by nature, he had little interest in domestic administration or the niceties of court life, and spent most of his
short reign, to 195 B.C., suppressing military challenges of
ambitious subordinates and fighting defensively against a
Turkic-speaking northern people known as the Hsiung-nu,
who had formed history's first great nomadic confederation in
Mongolia.

Kao-tsu was canny enough, however, to heed the warning
of an adviser that was to be repeated to dynastic founders
many times later: "You may have conquered the empire on
horseback, but you cannot rule it on horseback." He established a central government dominated by trusted aides, and
he set two precedents that have been greatly honored in the
Chinese heritage: policy proposals were to be initiated by
officials rather than by the emperor; and policy decisions
were to be made by the emperor only after widespread
consultation and deliberation among his ministerial advisers.

The new Han regime was a blend of pre-Ch'in feudalism
and Ch'in's autocratic centralism. Kao-tsu parceled out the
eastern half of the empire to relatives and generals in semi-
feudal, semi-autonomous, hereditary fiefs in two categories of
rank, princedoms and marquisates. The western half he
divided Ch'in-style into commanderies and subordinate districts, the commanderies being governed by nonhereditary
but powerful appointees of the central government. Land
everywhere was freely bought and sold, Ch'in laws and taxes
were moderated, and laissez-faire attitudes prevailed at the
capital, which was built on the ruins of Ch'in's capital in
Shensi and was now optimistically named Ch'ang-an (Prolonged Peace).

The central government on the whole was something like
an imperial household administration, but as in Ch'in times it
controlled large military forces garrisoned around the capital, and in its highest echelon it had three dignitaries with
empire-wide responsibilities. There were a chief commander
of the military; a chief counselor, or prime minister, supervis-

ing a group of functionally differentiated agencies; and a censor-in-chief who assisted the chief counselor and had a staff of censors who made inspection tours of the empire and could impeach officials of any rank. The system was of a type traditionally characterized as a strong prime ministership. It produced a series of influential officials who did not shrink from remonstrating vigorously with emperors they considered wrong-minded.

The semi-feudal character of the early Han state made it possible for several imperial princes to organize a serious rebellion in 154 B.C. The central government proved strong enough to suppress this challenge promptly, and thereafter the semi-autonomous status of the princedoms and marquisates was altered to prevent further trouble. Administrators were sent from Ch'ang-an to take charge of all fiefs under the supervision of the chief counselor. From then on, although the lords retained rights to part of the state revenues collected in their titular fiefs, the princedoms and marquisates were close counterparts of the commanderies and districts elsewhere.

Emperor Wu

Under the laissez-faire policies established by Kao-tsu, the first 60 years of Han rule gave the Chinese an opportunity to recuperate from the turbulence of the Warring States era and the harshness of Ch'in. The population grew, the economy expanded, and culture flourished. State granaries and treasuries bulged. The Chinese mood was proud, confident, and restless when there came to the throne a new ruler who by temperament was well suited to the time. This was Wu-ti, or Emperor Wu, who reigned over China from 141 to 87 B.C., longer than anyone else until the eighteenth century. Vigorous, imaginative, and bold, he dominated the government and took major initiatives that changed Chinese history.

Centralization of power. Mindful of the recent rebellion of seven princes, Emperor Wu set out early to humble the nobility completely and assert his personal power. Summoning nobles to court, he required them to present him gifts of white deerskin of a type that was obtainable only at the imperial treasury, at exorbitant prices. On the slightest pretexts he stripped lords of their status, confiscated their wealth, and transformed their nominal fiefs into ordinary commanderies and districts. Most insidiously and effectively, he decreed that every princedom and marquisate must be divided on the lord's death among all his sons, equally, through every generation. By the end of Emperor Wu's reign the nobility had been reduced to powerless adornments of the state. This new campaign of defeudalization was continued by Emperor Wu's successors, so that by the end of Former Han not a single heir of the founding emperor's nobility retained noble status.

War and expansion. After Kao-tsu's reign, the Chinese chose to appease the Hsiung-nu in the north rather than challenge them, and for more than a generation peace was bought by regular Chinese gifts of grain and silk and occasional presentations of marriageable Han princesses to nomad chiefs. As China's domestic conditions stabilized, however, Han generals began chafing in impatience to strike out against the Hsiung-nu, and both state and private mercantile groups grew irritated at Hsiung-nu disruptions in Central Asia. Already camel caravans were bringing China such luxury goods as fine-quality jade in exchange for Chinese silk bound for the Mediterranean world. Emperor Wu readily agreed with the advisers who urged vigorous action to assert and defend China's interests. In 139 b.c. he dispatched the courtier Chang Ch'ien westward to scout out conditions and find anti-Hsiung-nu allies. Chang was gone 13 years, twice being captured by Hsiung-nu, but he ultimately returned with valuable strategic information.

Meanwhile, beginning in 133 b.c. Emperor Wu sent armies northward from Ch'ang-an to oust the Hsiung-nu from the Ordos plateau in northern Shensi, a prized staging base from

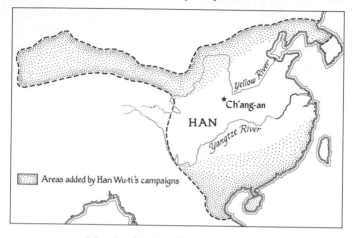

Map 2. The Han Empire, c. 100 B.C.

which they had raided Shensi and Shansi at will. By 127 the Ordos had been retaken and resettled with Chinese, and by 119 campaigns westward from the Ordos had cleared the Hsiung-nu out of modern Kansu, China's gateway to Central Asia. Many thousands of Chinese colonists were eventually settled in Kansu, and the Great Wall was extended to Tun-huang at the eastern end of the great Chinese Turkestan desert, the traditional junction of Central Asian caravan routes. Then, in 108, armies from Kansu began leapfrogging out among the oasis statelets encircling the desert, establishing military colonies as small peacekeeping units. In campaigns from 104 to 101 B.C. Han generals led forces across the Pamirs into Russian Turkestan, in the farthest western extension of Emperor Wu's authority. In the final decades of his reign the Hsiung-nu successfully harassed the western regions anew, but to the end of Former Han the court at Ch'ang-an managed to uphold the prestige that Emperor Wu had gained throughout Chinese Turkestan.

This proud emperor also thrust his influence into the south, the southwest, and the northeast. Ch'in's collapse had left Chinese adventurers and native chiefs in command of the south coastal regions, and the early Han emperors had been content not to be bothered with them. But in 112 B.C., partly coveting the pearls, ivory, and spices that came from the south, Emperor Wu mounted a major campaign against the principal southern state—Nan Yüeh (Nam Viet), which had its capital at Canton—and by the end of the next year had won control over the southern littoral. Han commanderies spread throughout the south, including modern North Vietnam; and sea trade with the Southeast Asian island peoples began to thrive. By 109 B.C. the Yunnan plateau of the inland southwest, rich in tin and other minerals, had also been brought under Chinese administration.

Emperor Wu's armies campaigned northeast of China Proper, in modern Manchuria, in 109–108 B.C. Their successes resulted in the establishment of Han commanderies extending to modern Pyongyang, the capital of North Korea. Like Vietnam in the south, Korea now began to absorb Chinese culture; and through Korea the Chinese began to learn about Japan, then still in a neolithic stage of development.

The tributary system. Emperor Wu's military conquests in Central Asia are especially notable because they created a pattern of international relations that was to be a Chinese characteristic throughout subsequent imperial history. It was important to China (a) to keep the Central Asian caravan routes open for trade; (b) to this end, to keep the Central Asian oasis peoples and the Hsiung-nu of the area submissive; and (c) to keep the Hsiung-nu of the north from harassing the North China homeland. The barren lands of the west and north, however, were not suited to the kind of agricultural development that could support substantial sedentary populations, which were essential for the sort of expansion that was incorporating South China. The Chinese were never able to make their settlements in the west and north more than small, largely self-sufficient garrisons, and even then these garrisons were able to survive only with the tolerance and support of the native peoples of the oases and the steppes.

In dealing with these areas that could not be incorporated under commandery administrations, the Chinese in Emperor Wu's time developed what came to be known as a tributary system—an extension abroad of somewhat feudalistic arrangements, which were simultaneously being replaced within China by nonfeudal centralization. Local leaders— oasis kings and steppe khans—who submitted to China's generals were allowed to retain their status and to govern in local customary fashion so long as they kept the peace, accepted symbols of Han overlordship, and assisted Han armies when called on. Rulers' sons were customarily sent to Ch'ang-an to be educated in the Chinese style and, no doubt, to serve as hostages guaranteeing the good conduct of their fathers; and Chinese princesses or noblewomen were often given in marriage to the alien rulers. The non-Chinese chiefs generally found such arrangements as advantageous as the Chinese did. Their prestige and security at home were strengthened by Han's recognition and support, and the price demanded by Han was not exorbitant.

This system of relationships matured soon after Emperor Wu's reign. In 59 B.C. an imperial commissioner was appointed to oversee and coordinate China's diplomatic and military activities in Central Asia, as a kind of viceroy comparable to Rome's proconsuls in the distant parts of its empire. It was considered proof of the success of the system when, in 51 B.C., a leading Hsiung-nu khan paid a state visit to the Ch'ang-an court.

State economic management. Another important precedent that was established in Emperor Wu's reign was the adoption of aggressive state policies to control the national economy. The reasons for these actions were social as well as economic in nature. Since Ch'in times state fiscal policies had been keyed to agricultural production. Merchants as a class were thought to be nonproductive parasites and as a matter of policy had been discouraged, discriminated against, and restricted to doing business in designated marketplaces under the eyes of state officials. Yet by Emperor Wu's time merchants who were forbidden by law to ride in carriages or wear silk were in fact becoming wealthy and arrogant. As in Warring States times, this was especially true of grain speculators, iron manufacturers, and salt dealers. Emperor Wu's military campaigns were meantime draining away the once large treasury surpluses. He was easily persuaded to launch a many-faceted attack on the merchant class, designed to rectify its violations of the ordained social order and, no doubt more importantly, to capture its wealth for the state. The principal fiscal innovations were:

1. Merchant families were forbidden to own land.

2. Taxes in cash were imposed on merchant wagons and boats, and tax evaders had all their property confiscated.

3. Ad valorem taxes were imposed on merchants' inventories, under the same threat of confiscation.

4. The state established so-called ever-normal granaries in all areas, which bought up surplus grain to keep prices from falling and sold grain at times and in areas of shortage to keep prices from rising. It was intended that in this way supplies and prices would be stabilized, private speculation and hoarding would be unprofitable, and the state would make a reasonable profit.

5. The manufacture of salt and iron was placed under state control by license, and wholesale distribution was monopolized by state agencies. Private profiteering in these essential products was thus stopped, and such profits as were made accrued to the state.

State economic controls on such a scale were not without their critics and were not consistently enforced. But they amounted to a very ambitious program asserting the right and obligation of the state to intervene actively in the marketplace to its own benefit and also to prevent the private exploitation of either producers or consumers. This principle was part of China's political theory from this time on.

The beginnings of bureaucracy. In the earliest Han years, as seems to have been the case in Ch'in times, men were appointed to government office on the basis of recommendations by existing officials. In an effort to recruit new men, Kao-tsu, in 196 B.C., ordered all local officials to recommend "worthy and talented" men of their acquaintance for appointment. In 165 B.C. all court ministers, as well as princes, marquises, and commandery governors, were ordered to recommend new men capable of "speaking out forthrightly and remonstrating without inhibition," and the emperor himself gave written examinations to all nominees—probably the first written examinations of any sort in world history. During Emperor Wu's reign these precedents were developed into systematic personnel-recruitment practices. Furthermore, in 124 B.C. the emperor instituted a rudimentary national university specifically for the training of future officials. Its faculty consisted of officials of the central government called Erudites, each a specialist in one of the Five Classics, and the students were promising youths recommended by local authorities. At first there were just 50 students; but the system grew very rapidly, until by the end of Former Han enrollment had reached 3,000.

From Emperor Wu's time on, then, there were two paths open for recruitment into the civil officialdom on the basis of individual merit: (a) recommendation by local authorities leading directly to a confirmatory examination in the capital, success in which gave one status as an expectant official awaiting a vacancy; and (b) recommendation by local authorities leading to enrollment in the national university, successful completion of a designated curriculum there giving one similar status as an expectant official. Beginning in Emperor Wu's reign, calls for recommendations of both types were issued annually, and each commandery was required to submit one or two nominees. After Emperor Wu's time, most middle- and low-ranking officials seem to have been produced by these recommendation processes, and it can fairly be said that China was largely administered by literate, bureaucratic careerists.

Nevertheless, and despite the fact that men of very humble social status sometimes skyrocketed into eminence, it must be kept in mind that the Han civil service was not what we would consider democratic. Recruitment required literacy, and literacy was almost necessarily restricted to those few whose families were wealthy enough to hire tutors and have access to books, which were available only in expensive handwork copies on wooden slats or silk. The system also required that one be recommended by local authorities, who were certainly not likely to recommend anyone not of good breeding—that is, anyone outside the small circle of great families that dominated every area. Thus being wealthy may not have guaranteed or have been an official requirement for winning office and political power, but offices were seldom won by men without wealthy family backgrounds. In the Han system, moreover, many officials could appoint their own subordinates; some could appoint their own successors, and almost any official of substance could have one or more of his sons granted status as expectant officials without undergoing any special recruitment procedures. Still, the establishment of a system for recruiting appropriate talents for government service in a regular fashion must be reckoned a major Han achievement, in which Emperor Wu conspicuously shared.

Former Han Culture

Urbanization, which had been a notable trend in the Warring States era, stabilized under Han rule. In A.D. 1 the registered population of the administrative area that included the national capital, Ch'ang-an, was 246,200; probably some 80,000 resided within the capital's walls. A dozen or so other towns were considered large, as had been the case in the last Chou centuries. Thus although the Former Han population reached a total of some 60,000,000, no more than 1,000,000 could have been urban residents. The aristocratic elite of noble and other great families were not wholly town-oriented.

The material remains left from Former Han times indicate that the elite nevertheless lived an opulent life. Their tombs were often lavishly provided with pottery miniatures of their houses, servants, animals, and entertainers. Tombs were also often decorated with painted tiles or murals sculpted in low relief, depicting important events in a representational spirit that might be called stylized realism. Literary evidence suggests that the walls of palaces and great private residences were customarily covered with painted portraits and scenes, but none of these remain. Jade carvings and round mirrors cast in bronze, with shiny reflecting surfaces and decorated backs, were also among the admired art forms of the age.

Bibliomania. The predominant cultural interest of Former Han times, however, was books. This was due partly to the widespread destruction of books by Ch'in and partly to the emphasis on literacy and education in the developing civil service recruitment procedures. The government and great private families both strove to reconstruct and perpetuate old works that had been lost, and different texts became current in some instances. It was relatively easy to fabricate texts and attribute them to pre-Ch'in antiquity, and it was possibly during the early Han years that such long venerated classics as the *Chou Rituals* (*Chou-li*), the *Ritual Records* (*Li-chi*), the appendixes or "wings" interpreting the *Classic of Changes* (*I-ching*), and some of the commentaries on the *Spring and Autumn Annals* (*Ch'un-ch'iu*) were actually written. The elite developed a passion for copying and collecting books—a bibliomania that remained characteristic of educated Chinese into our own times; and there began arguments about the authenticity of ancient works that have never been satisfactorily resolved.

Literature. Early Han additions to the literary heritage notably included new types of poetry and of historiography. In poetry the song form called *shih* that dominates the *Classic of Songs* (*Shih-ching*) remained standard, with its thumpety-thump, four-beat lines, its normal four-line stanzas, and its general brevity and simplicity. But in the earliest Han years the esteem of the *Classic of Songs* was rivaled by that of a late Chou collection called the *Elegies of Ch'u* (*Ch'u-tz'u*). About half of the collection is traditionally attributed to the first identifiable major poet of Chinese history, Ch'ü Yüan, a member of the royal clan of the southern state of Ch'u who committed suicide by drowning not later than 265 B.C. All the songs are ascribed to southerners, and all differ markedly from the North China songs represented in the *Classic of Songs,* both in form and in spirit. These are irregular verses, with a seven-word line predominating, stretching to much greater length than the old shih; and they reveal an enchantment with words, an ornate imaginativeness, and a penchant for lugubrious lamentation. The *Elegies of Ch'u* is considered a great literary treasure, exuding what we might call a romantic lyricism that is uncharacteristic of the *Classic of Songs.*

The new poetic spirit infused Han poems called *fu,* which are long, irregular, verbose, elaborately ornate descriptive prose-poems about events or people or such things as gardens and parks. The greatest fu master was a roguish adventurer of Emperor Wu's time, Ssu-ma Hsiang-ju.

Another new poetic form that now appeared was the *yüeh-fu.* This was the name of a governmental agency, the Music Bureau, transferred to a type of poetry associated with it. The bureau provided music for state ceremonial occasions and also collected songs that were popular among the common folk, since these were traditionally believed to provide a kind of public opinion poll that measured the mood of the people and, consequently, the effectiveness of the ruler's policies. Yüeh-fu poems were freer in form than the old shih, but simpler in form and spirit than the elaborate fu. Yüeh-fu quickly became the medium in which poets expressed their personal emotions—as, for example, in love lyrics.

In historiography the Han official Ssu-ma Ch'ien (145–87 B.C.?) was China's first identifiable major figure, and he has won recognition as one of the greatest, most innovative, and most influential historians the world has produced. Inheriting his father's court post as Lord Grand Astrologer, which gave him access to court archives, he carried to completion a project initiated by his father—a history of the world up to his time (the world as known to him and to China, of course). The resulting work, called the *Historical Records* (*Shih-chi*), is a masterpiece of both organization and style. Its 130 chapters include, in addition to a chronology of important events from the legendary Yellow Emperor down into Emperor Wu's reign, chronological tables for easy reference, historical treatises on topics such as music, the calendar, and waterways, and most important, hundreds of biographies of prominent or interesting people, the notorious as well as the famous. Ssu-ma Ch'ien established a pattern for organizing historical data that was used subsequently in a series of so-called dynastic histories, which preserve the history of imperial China in unsurpassed detail and uniquely systematic order. Moreover, Ssu-ma's lively style made his work a literary monument that has been read with delight by educated classes throughout East Asia.

Thought. Early Han thought, even in the most learned circles, was a hodgepodge of folk superstitions, yang-yin and other pseudoscientific cosmological speculations based on the *Classic of Changes,* and fanciful cult myths about gods and goddesses who presided over mystical isles and heavenly realms and could confer immortality on their favorites. Most such beliefs were taught by professed Taoists, who by this time had degenerated into little more than shamanistic charlatans. Legalism, though a major influence on the structure and workings of Han government, was virtually taboo because of its association with Ch'in. Confucianism, having long since lost the moderate conservative reformist character given it by Confucius and his early followers, was a bookish creed preoccupied with funerals, mourning, and other ritual matters.

Confucianism was revived as a philosophical force by the scholar Tung Chung-shu (c. 179–104 B.C.), who so impressed Emperor Wu that he pronounced Confucianism the ideological basis of the state, declared only professed Confucians to be eligible for state office, and made Confucianism the curriculum of the national university. It has consequently been common for Western students to say that Emperor Wu's reign marked "the triumph of Confucianism" and to describe the governmental system that evolved out of Emperor Wu's time as being "the Confucian state."

Tung Chung-shu was Confucian because he believed he was an interpreter of Confucius for his own time, and because he endorsed the major ethical principles of the early Confucians: filial piety, loyalty, a sense of right, courtesy, human-kindness, and the like. He even reconciled the differences between Mencius and Hsün-tzu concerning human nature by insisting with Mencius that every man is potentially good but believing like Hsün-tzu that goodness must be developed by disciplined training and practice. Two aspects of his thought must have made it irresistible to Emperor Wu. First, he justified Confucian ethics and politics by cosmological explanations incorporating all the current pseudoscientific fads; he made the *Classic of Changes* a Confucian canon, and yang and yin essential elements of the Confucian ideology. Second, he idealized and aggrandized the role of the ruler, suggesting that the written character for the word king, *wang* 王 , itself testifies that it is the ruler who (as indicated by the vertical stroke) unifies Heaven, Man, and Earth (the three horizontal strokes). Tung also argued that only the charismatic influence of the ruler could cause people to develop the potential goodness in them.

It was this concept of kingship, and not any notion of Confucius and his early followers, that was the foundation of the state ideology throughout the rest of imperial history. Though it made the ruler the earthly agent of Heaven's will, it fell short of deifying him. As a matter of fact, Tung Chung-shu—and later Confucians—accepted astronomical phenomena and aberrations in nature's normal course as signs of Heaven's displeasure; and on such grounds they made life miserable for many emperors, persuading them that the responsibility for all the world's ills lay on the ruler's shoulders and causing rulers to prostrate themselves penitently at the altar of Heaven. Thus the power of being Father and Mother of the People was counterbalanced in some measure by the awesome burden of being Son of Heaven. However easy it may have been for Emperor Wu to ignore such ideological constraints on his authority, generations of daring and conscientious officials made sure that later rulers understood it.

Wang Mang

After Emperor Wu's death in 87 B.C. China was not seriously menaced by the Hsiung-nu, the population and the economy expanded, culture flourished, and there seems to have been a general relaxation. The ruling Liu family, however, produced no more strong leaders. The court reverted to the laissez-faire attitudes of earlier times and devoted itself to intrigues involving domineering imperial in-laws. After a succession of young emperors died without leaving natural heirs, courtiers began suggesting that the Han dynasty must have run its Heaven-ordained course. In A.D. 6 an infant was put on the throne under a regency council, and in A.D. 9 he was set aside in favor of a prestigious minister, Wang Mang, who is one of the most fascinating and controversial figures of imperial history.

Wang was originally an obscure member of a powerful family of imperial in-laws. His connections and his reputation as a man of virtue enabled him to rise into ever higher offices, and when he accepted the throne he seemed a genuinely popular choice to found a new dynasty; some even pronounced him a new Duke of Chou. He called his dynasty Hsin, meaning "new," and promptly set about reviving institutions ascribed to the early Chou era in a campaign to achieve what he considered a Confucian utopia. His reform decrees were of astonishing scope and audacity:

1. He vastly expanded the titled nobility with Wang-family appointees, conferred on the new nobles some of the feudal powers described in the *Chou Rituals*, and shuffled the titles that had been given alien tributary chiefs.

2. He reinstated discriminatory policies against merchants, made them harsher than before, and imposed a regular income tax on artisans and merchants.

3. He forbade the sale and purchase of slaves and tried to alleviate the conditions of slavery in general. (Convicts had often been made state slaves, and many desperate peasants had sold their children or themselves into slavery. Slaves numbered perhaps 1,000,000 at most.)

4. He reasserted the ancient doctrine that all land is the king's land, prohibited its sale and purchase, undertook an equitable distribution of land by confiscating the excess holdings of the wealthy without compensation, and in general foresaw a restoration of the well-field system attributed to the Chou dynasty.

5. He confiscated all gold, instituted a new coinage having no relation to the intrinsic value of coins, and successively devalued money—apparently in an effort to destroy hoarded wealth.

6. Justifying himself by new interpretations of vague passages in the classics and disregarding traditional Confucian disapproval, he revived Emperor Wu's state economic controls under new names and then expanded them so as to create a system of almost total state regulation of natural resources, marketing, and even credit, using the new tax revenues from artisans and merchants to fund state loans to needy peasants.

Wang Mang's reform package was the most dramatic innovation attempted by any Chinese ruler up to his time. It seems to have been partly a sincere effort to help the common people at the expense of the wealthy, partly a hardheaded effort to increase state income, and partly an outburst of utopian idealism. Unfortunately for Wang, his reforms were abortive. Few proved enforceable even for a short time, primarily because the officials called on to enforce them represented the very class that would have suffered most from them. In the end, all classes seem to have been antagonized or disillusioned.

Nature also seemed to conspire against Wang Mang. There was a series of disastrous harvests. Perennial drought settled on the Shensi basin, where the capital was located. In A.D. 11 the Yellow River broke out of its dikes in the eastern end of the North China plain, inundated vast territories, and eventually changed its course to run south rather than north of the Shantung peninsula. The emperor's welfare schemes were inadequate to cope with the resultant problems, and refugees became outlaws and rebellious vagrants roaming across China. By A.D. 18 a great rebellion was under way, organized by malcontents known as the Red Eyebrows, and soon several rival members of the old Han ruling family were rallying armies to overthrow Wang. In A.D. 23 rebels broke into the palace and murdered him. Wang was thereafter vilified as a tyrannical usurper, and for hundreds of years the memory of his ruinous reign was dredged up as a deterrent against ambitious socioeconomic reform schemes.

Later Han

The Restoration

The rebellions that ended Wang Mang's turbulent reign led in A.D. 25 to the accession of a member of the Liu family, who restored the Han dynasty. Known as Emperor Kuang-wu (r. 25–57), he established a new dynastic capital at Loyang in Honan, near his own power base, and reinstituted the laissez-faire domestic policies of early Han. The population, which had shrunk dramatically in Wang Mang's time, quickly rebounded and regained its Former Han peak of about 60,000,000; and agriculture and commerce recovered from their recent disruptions. Han generals established Chinese influence even more firmly than before in northern Vietnam and Chinese Turkestan. The Hsiung-nu split into antagonistic groups and ceased troubling China. Trade to the south and west resumed their earlier growth, and the ruling elite basked in ever greater affluence. By the end of Han in 220, important innovations such as the breast-strap harness for draft animals, the wheelbarrow, tea, and paper were adding new dimensions to everyday life in China.

In government the recruitment techniques initiated in Former Han produced a more and more bureaucratic officialdom; by the second century enrollment in the national university swelled to 30,000, and there was a strong cohesive sense of professionalism in the administration. The strong prime ministership of Former Han had disappeared, however: the top echelon of the central government now consisted of (a) an uncoordinated staff of generals under the emperor's control; (b) a large Censorate maintaining disciplinary surveillance over the whole officialdom; and (c) three coordinate general-administration agencies—a Chancellery, a Secretariat, and a Department of State Affairs—whose ranking officials constituted a kind of council of state. The empire was now divided into 13 large regions or circuits, and commanderies were subordinate to the intermediary circuit intendants, who steadily became more powerful regional governors.

Great-Family Dominance

Even more markedly than in Former Han, a few powerful families now dominated both society and government. These were not extended families or clans, for Han had continued Ch'in policies that discouraged relatives from living together. The great family now, especially in Later Han, was something like a large, diversified business company owned by one powerful man and passed on to his heir. It controlled a vast tract of land incorporating many peasant villages, craft workshops, and mercantile establishments; it patronized hordes of so-called "guests," ranging from astrologers to scholarly protégés to political assassins; and it had its own army of mercenaries who manned fortifications that defended the family's domain from its rivals. Emperor Kuang-wu had emerged from such a great-family background, and his conservative policies made Later Han less a centralized nation than a coalition of local satrapies.

The small, free farmer idealized by both Confucians and Legalists in pre-Han times was by now disappearing rapidly from the rural scene. He simply could not long survive in a society dominated by land barons whose abuses the government did not try to restrain. He was easily squeezed into submission by his wealthy neighbors, becoming a serf-like tenant or even a slave.

Disillusion and Dissension

Growing pessimism. The failure of Wang Mang's attempted reforms in many realms not only doomed the peasantry to this steadily worsening condition; it seems to have soured the buoyant, optimistic confidence of the Former Han period. Emperor Kuang-wu fostered a sober, chastened realism, and this soon gave way to cynicism, fatalism, and finally escapism. The new mood was reflected in an intensification of the intellectuals' obsession with bookishness. A series of great commentators on the classics appeared in the first century—conservatively philological, not interested in social or political reformism.

Philosophically, the optimism of Tung Chung-shu was challenged by the first-century scholar-official Wang Ch'ung, who was very skeptical about man's ability to influence events in any way and about Heaven's inclination to requite good and evil appropriately. "Whether the world is well ordered or disordered is a matter of the time, not of policies," he wrote; "whether a state is safe or endangered is a matter of its destiny, not of its doctrines; and whether there are worthy or unworthy men or enlightened or unenlightened policies cannot change things for better or worse." Wang was followed by even more fatalistic thinkers, who combined lip-service to Confucianism with thoroughly Legalistic arguments for strong laws, strict enforcement, and harsh punishments. Other intellectuals revived Taoist naturalism, especially in an escapist movement of "pure chitchat." This movement endured beyond the end of Han, producing a famous group of wits and bon vivants called the Seven Sages of the Bamboo Grove, who renounced all personal responsibility for the state of society and gleefully flouted every convention. Totally pessimistic Buddhism, which came to China from India about the time of Christ and was beginning to find devotees at court and in elite circles elsewhere in the second century, could not but contribute to the growing disillusionment of Later Han.

Popular rebellions. Among commoners the new mood expressed itself in religious cults committed to catchall Taoist doctrines and organized into faith-healing, drug-dispensing, polytheistic Taoist churches that practiced congregational worship and preached individual escapism through the attainment of physical immortality. Especially following widespread epidemics in 173 and 179 and devastating floods and locust infestations in 175, thousands of peasants flocked to join such church groups. Two groups, the Yellow Turbans in eastern China and the Five Pecks of Rice Band in Szechwan, became so numerous by 182 that the government set out to suppress them. In response both groups declared open rebellion in 184.

Disarray at court. The central government was ill-prepared to cope with such problems because it had been beset with divisive factional struggles since A.D. 88, when a minor came to the throne. A succession of short-lived, weak emperors let power fall into the hands of dowager empresses and their abusive relatives. Then emperors turned in self-defense to their most intimate associates—palace eunuchs, who had recurrently played important political roles at court since Chou times. Normally castrated for vicious crimes and assigned to service in the imperial harem, eunuchs had unique opportunities to ingratiate themselves with emperors, and emperors often considered them the least defenseless and therefore the most trustworthy of their attendants. Civil service officials, in Later Han as always, were outraged by the machinations of both eunuchs and imperial in-laws, and poured out futile protests. National university students gathered in mass demonstrations at the palace supporting one "honest critic" after another. Beginning in 159 all these intrigues and confrontations led to a series of massacres.

Warlordism. While the central government was thus engaged, generals assigned to put down the Yellow Turban and related uprisings that exploded in 184 made themselves into autonomous regional warlords. In 190 one general seized Loyang, put to death the empress dowager and an imperial prince, slaughtered eunuchs wholesale, deposed the current emperor, and installed his own Liu-family protégé on the throne. A coalition of other warlords then turned on him, and soon a general named Ts'ao Ts'ao, who was himself the son of a palace eunuch's adopted son, seized the new emperor, became protector of the Han dynasty, finally put down the

Yellow Turban rebellion, and spent his last 20 years fighting inconclusively against rival warlords. He became one of the great legendary figures of Chinese history, remembered best in the saying, "Mention Ts'ao Ts'ao and Ts'ao Ts'ao arrives"— equivalent to our "Speak of the devil." When Ts'ao Ts'ao died in 220 his eldest son, in an elaborately planned ritualistic show of propriety, accepted the abdication of the last Han emperor and established a new dynasty called Wei. Thus Han, revered by later Chinese as the first great dynasty of the imperial heritage, came to an inglorious end after four centuries of dominance in East Asia.

The Era of Division

For four centuries following Han's decline into rampant warlordism in 190, with the exception of one short generation from 280 to 316, China was politically disunited. First, warlords carved the Han empire into three warring king-doms. Then, from 316 to 589, the country was divided roughly along the Tsinling Mountains between the Yellow and Yangtze rivers. A succession of weak dynasties in the south carried on the heritage of Han culture, and a succession of alien nomads dominated North China. The whole era has traditionally been considered by the Chinese an unfortunate and disesteemed interlude, much as modern Europeans have thought of their so-called Dark Ages of medieval times. But in China, as in Europe, it was actually a time of fundamental importance in reshaping the mainstream of civilization. At both ends of the Eurasian continent new blood and new customs were being absorbed into, and were transforming, the previously dominant "classical" culture; new patterns of political and social organization were being developed; and new forms of thought, literature, and art were emerging. It was a confusingly disordered age, to be sure; but it was vibrant with institutional and cultural ferment of the utmost importance. Most notably, perhaps, just as Christianity was

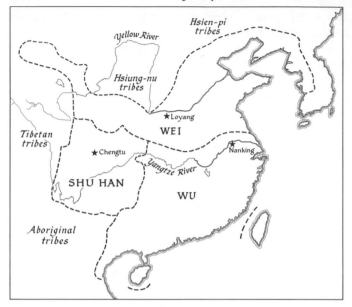

Map 3. The Three Kingdoms, c. 230

overwhelming Graeco-Roman paganism in Europe, so Buddhism was overwhelming Han Confucianism in China.

Political Chaos

When Ts'ao Ts'ao's son established his Wei dynasty at Loyang in 220, he was in actual control of only the North China homeland. Two rivals promptly proclaimed themselves emperors elsewhere, creating a Shu Han state with its capital at Chengtu, which controlled Szechwan and parts of the highland southwest, and a Wu state with its capital at Nanking, which controlled the rest of the Yangtze River watershed and the coastal areas south into Vietnam. Wei, Shu Han, and Wu fought each other in a continuation of Ts'ao Ts'ao's struggles with his antagonists, and the so-called Three Kingdoms era subsequently was regarded as a romantic epoch of knightly derring-do, the historical source of much later fiction and drama, much like the great age of chivalry in medieval Europe. Among the more esteemed personages of the time were Kuan Yü (d. 219), a brave, strong, and loyal warrior, who was later canonized as China's god of war, and Chu-ko Liang (d. 234), chief counselor of Shu Han, who won renown as the wiliest of diplomatic and military strategists.

The northern state of Wei eventually prevailed, absorbing Shu Han in 263 and conquering Wu in 280. Meantime, however, the authority of the ruling Ts'ao family had been whittled away by generals of the Ssu-ma family, and in 265 a Ssu-ma had usurped the throne and changed Wei into the Chin dynasty. It was under Chin rule that China was reunited in 280.

China's prolonged civil wars had given the nomadic northern peoples the opportunity to revive their earlier ambitions, and the introduction of the stirrup on the steppes made them a stronger force, as heavily armored cavalry. Although some Hsiung-nu had long since drifted westward out of China's world to reemerge in Europe as the Huns of Attila, others had occupied northern Shansi and Shensi in a nominal vassal status since early in Later Han and had become semi-Sinicized. Declaring themselves the rightful heirs of Han, these Hsiung-nu attacked and pillaged Chin's capitals at Loyang and Ch'ang-an in 311 and 316, respectively. Chinese refugees streamed southward and established a new Chin capital at Nanking, while ephemeral alien statelets known collectively as the Sixteen Kingdoms were established in different parts of North China—by Hsiung-nu, by proto-Tibetans, and by proto-Mongol Hsien-pi tribes.

After 316 two quite different societies developed in the north and the south, though both used Han as their model since no other model for a sedentary, centralized state was at hand. In the south an earlier mixture of Ch'in and Han settlers with aboriginal tribespeople was now mixed further with new Han Chinese refugees from the north. In the north the Han Chinese who remained gradually mixed with the conquering non-Chinese from Mongolia, who varied in their willingness to accommodate themselves to Chinese ways. Political fragmentation characterized both regimes; regicides, abdications, and usurpations kept all governments unstable and weak, and there were rapid changes of dynasties. Occasional attempts by one side or the other to reunify China Proper were humiliating failures.

Whereas the governments in South China became steadily weaker, North China began a recovery of stability in the late 400's under the leadership of tribes called T'o-pa (Toba), proto-Turks who were originally subservient allies of the Hsien-pi. The T'o-pa were dogged innovators in efforts to strengthen the state, and new institutions they devised made it possible for a northern dynasty, Sui (581–618), to crush the last Nanking-based dynasty in 589. Thus at last China was reunited, and a new age of splendor rivaling Han could dawn.

Neo-feudalism

The breakdown of government at all levels and the social disorder brought about by civil wars, alien invasions, and mass migrations in the late Han and post-Han years intensified the neo-feudal tendencies of Later Han. People increasingly gathered for protection into great-family estates, and autonomous local baronies became the normal structure of real sociopolitical power. Alien invaders of the north fitted easily into this pattern, tribal chieftains settling into roles comparable to those of the Chinese land barons. Both north and south, the common people became more rigidly subordinate, and elite families became more self-consciously aware of and protective toward their prerogatives. Intermarriage between classes was forbidden by custom and sometimes by law, and upward mobility became more difficult than ever before. Society became so stratified that some have compared it with the caste system of India.

The hereditary landowning elite, who called themselves

shih (the ancient term for warrior-officials), more than ever monopolized political power. They began compiling genealogical records to keep clear who was and who was not a shih. The tribal chiefs of the northern nomads assumed status as shih and even invented genealogies tracing their ancestry back to great men of China's past, especially Han ministers and generals. It became the rule that only shih of certified honorable ancestry were eligible for appointment in the government.

Thus social stratification hardened, and localities became more than ever self contained, self-sufficient, independent enclaves suspicious of all outside interference. States were very loose aggregations of such enclaves, and official appointments merely confirmed de facto hereditary status. One of the great achievements of the T'o-pa rulers in the north during the fifth and sixth centuries was to establish new patterns of land tenure and service obligations, which made possible a stable consolidation of North China and, under Sui, the conquest of the south. T'o-pa experiments of these sorts became the foundation stones of the new national stability, growth, and flourishing that marked the early years of the T'ang dynasty, described below.

Buddhism

In both north and south during the long era of division, Confucianism as reinterpreted in Han times remained the working ideology of state officials, the ethical principles that guided everyday life in the family and community, and the curriculum of such state-inspired education as existed. Han-style Neo-Taoism also survived as a mixture of intellectual naturalism, alchemy and other pseudosciences, popular church worship of many kinds of deities, and eccentric individualism of the "pure chitchat" variety. But these two traditions came to be overshadowed, in both elite and folk circles, by Buddhism.

Buddhism originated in India about the time of Confucius

and brought into China conceptions and practices from the Indian tradition that were dazzlingly new to the Chinese. The most important of these were:

1. An elaborate cosmology based on the view that the world perceptible to the human senses is illusory, concealing the true reality beyond.

2. Samsara, or the notion that living creatures experience many lifetimes, being reborn after every death into a new status.

3. Karma, or the assumption that the status into which one is reborn after any death is determined almost automatically by a computer-like balancing of merits and demerits accumulated by good and bad deeds during all previous existences.

4. The goal of escaping from the endless cycle of rebirths, or finding salvation, by realizing that there is no cosmic soul or god, there is no human soul or "real me," and rebirth comes only because of our selfish desires, including the subconscious desire to perpetuate the self. Such realization leads to a state of saintliness in which one knows one will not be reborn and at the end of this life will be "snuffed out" (nirvana)—not into utter extinction, but into a self-realization and fulfillment that is beyond human comprehension.

5. The belief that some saints, out of compassion for their fellow creatures, postpone their own entrance into nirvana upon death, linger in heavenly paradises that offer temporary respite from the cycle of rebirths, and offer their help as personal saviors to the living. Called bodhisattvas, these demigods include Amitabha, who presides over the most popular way-station to nirvana, called the Western Paradise; Kuan-yin, goddess of mercy; and Maitreya, a Buddha yet to come who is expected to establish a paradise on earth.

6. Monastic communities supported by devout lay congregations, in which monks and nuns who had renounced all worldly attachments and material belongings devoted themselves intensively to attaining salvation.

7. An extensive Buddhist literature, including canonical

texts of the original Buddha's teachings, learned expositions of Buddhist doctrines, and lively tales about the life of the Buddha and his adventures in many incarnations.

8. An impressive tradition of art, principally painting and statuary, emphasizing representations of the Buddha and his disciples, the bodhisattvas and their devotees, and the awesome creatures that inhabit various Buddhist paradises and purgatories.

In India Buddhism had developed two major schools: (a) Theravada (Doctrine of the Elders), which emphasized that only monks could find salvation, and (b) Mahayana (The Greater Vehicle), encompassing both elitist sects devoted to meditation and populist sects devoted to the worship of bodhisattvas, which taught that anyone could find salvation. (Mahayanists knew Theravada Buddhism by the deprecatory name Hinayana, "The Lesser Vehicle.") Both schools were introduced into China, but the Mahayana sects multiplied and eventually became paramount.

Buddhism was brought to China first by Indian missionaries coming by sea from the south and by Indian and Central Asian missionaries traveling overland. Gradually, however, Chinese pilgrims returning from Buddhism's holy places in India became the major innovators in Chinese Buddhism, and by the end of the era of division native monks and nuns were in charge everywhere. Rulers both north and south were converts and patrons, and Chinese Buddhist sects had been transplanted in Korea and Japan, where they became as influential as in China.

Buddhism's ethical teachings did not significantly conflict with traditional Confucian teachings, but monasticism drew Chinese out of their family-based sociopolitical nexus, and this troubled Chinese officials almost from the beginning. Moreover, even though rulers were the most lavish patrons of Buddhism, the fact that growing monastic estates took land off the tax rolls and exempted tenant farmers as well as monks from state service, including military conscription, caused the rulers of the northern dynasties to try to suppress or at least closely regulate Buddhist establishments, beginning as early as the 300's. Buddhist influence grew steadily nevertheless, even transforming the Chinese landscape with its monasteries, temples, pagodas, and grottoes. Taoists aped the Buddhists in this regard, establishing monasteries and temples of their own.

Literature and Art

Under alien domination after 316, North Chinese intellectuals specialized most notably in sober classical scholarship in the Han tradition, but in the south Chinese literature developed new fashions in both prose and poetry. The elegant rhyme-prose fu continued to flourish, and prose writing in general borrowed its elegance and ornateness, falling into a highly artificial "parallel prose" (*p'ien-wen*) style of alternating four- and six-word phrases, with irregular rhymes.

Fiction. At the same time there began to appear collections of less elegant prose pieces that mark the beginning of Chinese fiction as an independent genre; they no doubt perpetuated Han traditions of which we have no remaining examples. These are very simple short stories that mostly reflect traditional Taoist interests, dealing with ghosts, fairies, and marvels of all kinds. Buddhist preachers also contributed to the development of fiction by spicing up their sermons with marvelous tales out of their own tradition, relying heavily on the grammar and vocabulary of Chinese speech rather than of formal writing. Only scraps of these survive.

Poetry. The shih and yüeh-fu song forms of Han times continued to be written. One of their greatest early masters was a Taoist-inclined nature lover and recluse, T'ao Ch'ien, or T'ao Yüan-ming (365–427). The effete litterateurs of the southern dynasties, who seem to have spent their abundant leisure largely in "pure chitchat" sessions and versifying competitions, often wrote courtly love lyrics of an erotic nature that was not characteristic of any other period. An example is the following stanza from a set of poems called "Six Rememberings," by Shen Yüeh (441–513):

> I remember the times she slept—
> When others slept, trying not to doze.
> Loosening her gown, she needed no encouragement;
> On the pillows, she embraced ever more insistently.
> But afraid that her partner might be watching,
> She delicately blushed in the candlelight.

The most noteworthy poetic development of this age, however, was the introduction of so called "regulated shih." These are shih songs in five- or seven-word lines and normally two four-line stanzas that are subject to strict conventions about rhyme schemes, grammatical parallelism in couplets, and most especially, rigidly prescribed sequences of the tones in which Chinese words are pronounced. Composing a regulated shih is as unspontaneous as completing a crossword puzzle, and writing an abbreviated one-stanza form called the "stop-short" *(chüeh-chü)* is infinitely more rule-bound and demanding than doing an English sonnet or triolet.

The arts. The greatest art works that have survived from the era of division are Buddhist statues, which make this period China's great age of statuary. The most numerous and best preserved remains are in two famous cliff grottoes that were initiated under the patronage of T'o-pa rulers: Yün-kang in northern Shansi, where work began in 460, and Lung-men near Loyang, dating from 495. Later dynasties added to the original T'o-pa-era carvings in both places. Buddhist statues made of clay modeled over cores of wood or straw also adorn famous grottoes at Tun-huang and elsewhere in far northwestern China, favorite resting places for missionaries and pilgrims as well as traders. The 486 caves and niches at Tun-huang are most famous, however, for their elaborate, colorful Buddhist murals, which are the only significant remains of paintings from the era of division.

Sui

During the last century or so of the era of division the great families of Chinese who had remained in the north had begun to assert their political interests anew. One of them was a Yang family of Shensi, whose members became influential ministers under Hsien-pi and T'o-pa dynasties and intermarried with the ruling families. Yang Chien married a strong-willed alien noblewoman, became an eminent general and minister under the last of the so-called Northern Dynasties, the Northern Chou (557–81), and gave a daughter to the ruler in marriage. In 581 his infant grandson fell heir to the throne. Yang Chien allowed himself to be persuaded that the state needed more mature leadership. He set aside his grandson, took the throne himself as elder statesman, and proclaimed a new dynasty, Sui. Emperor Wen, as he is known, proved to be a prudent and effective ruler, and his armies succeeded in toppling the last Nanking-based dynasty, Ch'en, in 589.

Several things contributed to Emperor Wen's reunification of China. It was greatly to his advantage that Ch'en was a very weak state torn by factional intrigues. It was also fortuitous that a great nomad empire that had arisen in the 550's in Mongolia and Central Asia, and against which the T'o-pa rulers had to defend themselves vigorously, broke apart in 582 into two mutually antagonistic empires, eastern and western. These nomads were the Turks proper, whom the Chinese called T'u-chüeh; and their internal troubles freed Emperor Wen to throw most of his military strength into his southern campaigns.

But Emperor Wen was not merely favored by fate in these ways. He strengthened North China in preparation for the conquest of the south by his frugal policies, by building canals linking his capital at Ch'ang-an to the Yellow River and the fruitful North China plain, and by gathering the power of appointing all regular officials down to the district or county level into the hands of his central government, thus achieving a degree of centralized control not achieved even in Han times. Moreover, he tolerated and befriended Confucianism, Taoism, and Buddhism alike and used them all in propaganda aimed at pacifying all his subjects, north and south.

Emperor Wen's successes did not create instant national unity, peace, and prosperity; but they laid a solid foundation for later development. Unfortunately for the Chinese, progress was impeded by his son and successor, Emperor Yang, who gained the throne in 604 reportedly by poisoning his father and then embarked on a ruinously ambitious series of enterprises that quickly exhausted the state's resources, alienated the people, and caused later historians to judge him a vainglorious, tyrannical madman. He built a lavish new palace at Loyang and transferred the Sui capital there. He drafted laborers reportedly numbering more than 5,000,000 to finish a canal-building project begun by his father, linking the Yellow and Yangtze rivers via the natural waterways of east central China, and then had the system extended southward to Hangchow and northward to the Peking area. This is of course what Westerners know as China's Grand Canal, a truly monumental engineering achievement.

While this work was still in progress Emperor Yang raised new labor levies to repair and rebuild the Great Wall work in which more than 1,000,000 laborers are said to have died. He constructed a network of huge grain-storage depots in North China and built roads from the North China plain to the northern frontier zones. He also made a series of grandiose and costly inspection tours of China.

In addition, Emperor Yang conscripted armies that reconquered northern Vietnam and attacked the Cham people farther south, conducted exploratory expeditions to Taiwan, campaigned successfully against Turko-Mongol tribesmen of Chinese Turkestan, intimidated some Turkic nomads of Mongolia into accepting vassalage, and in three massive land and sea assaults in 612, 613, and 614 tried in vain to conquer the defiant Korean state of Koguryo.

When the unsuccessful campaigns against Koguryo were followed by a humiliating defeat at the hands of the Turks in the north in 615, Emperor Yang organized a grand expedition to take revenge on the Turks. He led it in person, with the result that in 617 his army was routed, and he himself was almost captured. Domestic revolts then sprang up everywhere. Ordering a frontier general known as the Duke of T'ang to deal with the rampaging Turks, Emperor Yang went to South China on an indefinite holiday and devoted himself to a life of leisure and licentiousness. In 618 he was assassinated by a courtier. By that time the Duke of T'ang had already renounced his allegiance and installed a puppet Sui heir at Ch'ang-an, and soon after Emperor Yang's death the Duke accepted his puppet's abdication and inaugurated the T'ang dynasty.

Because Sui became oppressively tyrannical, was short-lived, and gave way to a durable new dynasty that presided over a great flowering of Chinese culture and influence, it is commonly considered a latter-day Ch'in, and Emperor Yang is compared to the infamous First Emperor of Ch'in. As in the case of Ch'in and Han, however, it is probable that China could not have experienced the glories of T'ang without first enduring the exertions of Sui.

T'ang

The new ruling family symbolized the ethnic developments that had changed the meaning of "Chineseness" since Han times. The Duke of T'ang, whose personal name was Li Yüan and who is known by his posthumous temple designation Kao-tsu, on one side claimed descent from a famous Han general, but on the other side he was descended from northern aliens. Like the Northern Dynasties rulers, the early T'ang emperors were vigorous warrior-kings. After restoring the unity of China Proper, they spread China's military and political dominance farther across East and Central Asia than even Emperor Wu of Han; they had diplomatic relations

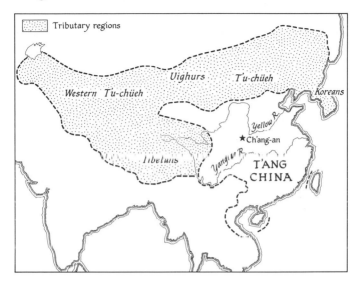

Map 4. The T'ang Empire, c. 700

with Persia and the Eastern Roman Empire at Constantinople; and it was in their time that the Japanese sent embassy after embassy to Ch'ang-an, borrowing wholesale from the institutions and culture of Chinese civilization.

The Early T'ang Rulers

Kao-tsu (r. 618–26) took over a Sui empire that was in shambles. More than 100 rivals were in the field, 11 of whom became serious challengers for supremacy. It was only by hard campaigning, and not until 624, that China Proper was again pacified. Meantime, Kao-tsu developed an effective administration and domestic policies in patterns partly derived from Han and partly pioneered by the T'o-pa and Sui rulers.

Kao-tsu's son T'ai-tsung (r. 626–49), whose personal name was Li Shih-min, has traditionally been considered the most nearly ideal emperor of the Chinese heritage. He was a wise, humane administrator who sought and heeded good counsel, and he was also a brilliant general. He personally led many of the armies that established T'ang superiority in China. Then he boldly ambushed and disposed of two jealous brothers, including the heir apparent, and finally he coerced Kao-tsu to retire in his favor when he was still only twenty-six years old. By 630 he so intimidated the Turks of Mongolia that they made him their grand khan; he was the first Chinese ruler to attain such power on the northern steppes. Campaigning westward in 639–40 and 647–48, his armies subjugated Chinese Turkestan, parts of Afghanistan beyond the Pamirs, and Tibet. In 648 a small Chinese force even crossed the forbidding Himalayas into northeastern India to chastise a regional ruler and brought him captive to Ch'ang-an. In the 640's T'ai-tsung also sent armies twice against Korea, but they met such firm resistance that they withdrew.

T'ai-tsung's son Kao-tsung (r. 649–83) allowed one of his father's young concubines to intrigue and poison her way to the status of empress and then to dominate the court, especially after his eyesight began to fail in 660. After his death she enthroned and deposed two of her sons in succession, and then, in 690, she took the throne herself, establishing a dynasty of her own with the venerable name Chou. This was one of the most powerful women of all Chinese history, known as Empress Wu; no other woman ever officially became emperor. She staffed the central and regional administrations with her relatives and others loyal to herself, but she carried on the general policies of the T'ang founders and maintained firm control over both domestic and foreign affairs. She even won grudging recognition as overlord from the aggressive state of Silla, which was unifying Korea. At the age of eighty, in 705, she was at last forced to abdicate by Li-family challengers.

After an unstable interlude of court intrigue, there came to the throne another of the most famous of all Chinese rulers,

Hsüan-tsung (r. 712–56). A conscientious, cultured, and extraordinarily gifted man, Hsüan-tsung presided over the T'ang empire in its golden age. Ch'ang-an became the world's greatest and most cosmopolitan metropolis, with a resident population of about 1,000,000 within the city walls. Musical troupes, jugglers, acrobats, dwarfs, and blacks from distant realms amused the crowds at the city's fairs; sing-song girls enlivened its eating and drinking houses with the newest tunes imported from Central Asia; and exotic wares from much of Eurasia, as well as specialty goods from every region of China, were sold in its markets. Hsüan-tsung's court was splendid beyond compare, adorned with scholars and litterateurs called to serve in a newly established and enduringly famous talent pool called the Hanlin Academy, entertained by theatrical performers trained in a new music and dance institute under imperial patronage. In Hsüan-tsung's reign flourished some of the greatest cultural geniuses of the Chinese tradition, among them the painter Wu Tao-tzu and the most renowned of all Chinese poets, Li Po and Tu Fu.

Early T'ang Institutions

The power and glory of High T'ang, from about 630 to 750, can be credited largely to domestic peace achieved by policies of tolerance and amnesty, to stability and prosperity achieved by vigorous governmental leadership, and to a national unity beyond any realized before. The Grand Canal made possible relatively easy transport and communication between north and south. The Chinese population, which had shrunk by half or more after the Han empire collapsed, rebounded to its Han peak of 60,000,000 and perhaps beyond; and great urban concentrations appeared, not only throughout the north, but to a lesser extent in the south also. In the eighth century 26 T'ang prefectures (successors of the Han commanderies, but far smaller and more numerous) had registered populations exceeding half a million. The south

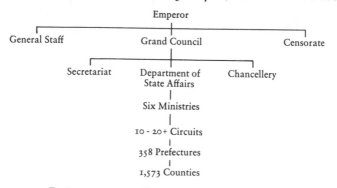

Basic governmental organization in T'ang times

was only beginning to come into its own, but Soochow and Hangchow in the southeast ranked among the most populous cities, and Arab visitors wrote admiringly of the cosmopolitan splendors of Canton, the south coast entrepot, and Yangchow at the confluence of the Grand Canal and the Yangtze.

Governmental structure. T'ang government evolved out of Han models, which all intervening dynasties had patterned themselves after, but it was much more complex and sophisticated. From T'ang times on to the end of China's imperial tradition, the administrative heart of the central government was a group of six ministries—of personnel, revenue, rites, war, justice, and works—which saw to the implementation of imperial policies at the local level, organized into prefectures and subordinate counties. In 711, in an effort to coordinate administration in larger regions, China Proper was divided into ten intermediary-level circuits, or proto-provinces, and the number and powers of the circuit intendants subsequently grew.

The principal government organs and their relationships are shown in the accompanying chart.

Civil service. T'ang personnel administration produced a more professional, bureaucratic officialdom than that of Han.

Two national universities were established, at Ch'ang-an and Loyang, and annual recruitment examinations were conducted, leading to a variety of degrees that we call doctorates. Candidates qualified for the examinations by their university work or by being recommended by prefects on the basis of screening examinations at the prefectural and county levels. Attaining a doctoral degree assured one of being considered for an appointment. But this was still not the only path to official status, or even the predominant path. High-ranking officials could still place their sons directly on the eligible list or in office, and members of families recognized by the government as being shih could be considered for any appointment. Moreover, no one could be admitted to the national universities or recommended for the examinations without being of shih status. Once appointed, however, civil officials now served for limited terms of duty in any office—normally three years—and were promoted and demoted, reappointed and dismissed, on the basis of merit ratings that superior officials now routinely submitted for their underlings and evaluations made by touring censors and the Ministry of Personnel. Thus, though the gate into officialdom was still narrow, a man's official career was considerably more subject to careful scrutiny than in Han times.

Fiscal administration. The basis of early T'ang fiscal stability was a system of land tenure and taxation called the "equal fields" (*chün-t'ien*) system. Similar in spirit to the idealized well-field system of antiquity, this was the end product of T'o-pa initiatives that had been further developed under Sui. Theoretically, farmlands were now allotted to families according to the number of their adult males. When a man died or reached old age, his allotment reverted to a state-controlled pool from which allocations were made annually to youths just reaching maturity. Taxes and state service levies could thus be imposed strictly on the basis of head counts, the assumption being that all families had equitable shares of land to work.

This principle seems to have been implemented satisfactorily for a time. But it could never be applied perfectly, and there were many deviations from the principle. Hereditary great families were never wholly stripped of their large estates; officials were allocated extra land while on duty and were allowed to pass much of their surplus holdings on to their heirs. Moreover, Buddhist and Taoist establishments were exempted from land limitations, taxation, and service obligations, so that peasants regularly commended their allotted lands to the church in arrangements that gave them de facto tax-free ownership. By the eighth century abuses of the system were seriously eroding the state fiscal order.

The military. Early T'ang military strength was largely due to another institution developed out of T'o-pa origins. This was a militia system called *fu-ping* (garrison soldiers), which encouraged men to enlist for lifetime military service in garrisons scattered strategically about the country and especially clustered in the northern frontier zones. Such service was not hereditary, and in early T'ang it had great prestige. Each garrison had an allocation of land, which its soldiers worked on part-time schedules so that the garrison was ideally self-supporting. In complicated rotational patterns, the garrisons sent men to serve as imperial guards at the capital, on defense duty along the Great Wall, and on active campaigns. The militiamen were supplemented in the defense of the capital by an elite army consisting of the original T'ang supporters and their heirs. In time, also, the border forces and attack troops had to be supplemented by mercenaries, often alien cavalrymen. As in the case of the equal-fields system, the militia system was in serious decline by the middle of the eighth century. Hsüan-tsung found it necessary to create great permanent frontier defense establishments along the Great Wall, each commanded by a powerful general, often of alien origin, controlling what amounted to a personal army of mercenaries.

Early T'ang Culture

The trends in religion, art, and literature that emerged in the era of division reached their culmination in early T'ang. Buddhism was at its zenith of intellectual dominance, sectarian diversification, and institutional influence. Its most intriguing Chinese product was a sect called Ch'an (Zen in Japanese), a blend of Buddhist and Taoist impulses. Ch'an monks worked at menial tasks to support themselves, sought salvation through nonrational inspiration rather than devout meditation on canonical texts, conceived of true reality as being nothing more than Here and Now perceived without the interposition of intellectuality, and included many individualistic eccentrics of the Taoist sort.

The arts. Buddhist statuary and painting continued to develop and thrive under the patronage of the court, great families, and humble devotees. Secular portraiture and mural art also flourished. Wu Tao-tzu (c. 700-760) gained renown as perhaps the greatest painter of Chinese history, working zestfully in a spirit of free personal expression. Landscape painting was becoming a respected art form. Very few T'ang paintings of any sort survive, however, so that we can judge them only by what admirers wrote of them.

Ceramics are the T'ang art forms best known to modern Westerners. Chinese artisans now began to produce true high-fired porcelain wares. But their most familiar products are relatively rough clay figurines decorated with paint or colored glazes. Spirited, prancing horses were a favorite product of T'ang ceramicists, and they are greatly admired throughout the world today.

Literature. T'ang was an age of great historians, classical commentators, and encyclopedists. It is especially renowned, however, as China's greatest age of poetry. Eighth-century T'ang abounded with memorable poets who excelled in all the forms inherited from the past and adopted new ones,

especially an irregular lyric form called the *tz'u*. Two poets of
the time stand head and shoulders above all others of China's
entire history, venerated by Chinese and outsiders alike.
They were contemporaries and friends, though quite different in temperament. Li Po (701-62) was the quintessential
Taoist free spirit, who tossed off complicated poems with
complete ease sober or drunk; who reveled in wine, women,
and song; and who blithely traveled about China proclaiming
himself "an immortal banished from Heaven." Something of
his gay spirit is caught in the following "stop-short":

The Girl of Yüeh

A girl picking lotuses beside the stream—
At the sound of my oars she turns about.
Giggling, she vanishes among the flowers,
And, all pretenses, declines to come out.

Tu Fu (712–70) was a more sober poetic craftsman and was
more conscientiously Confucian in his outlook. His poems are
less lyrical and more erudite than Li Po's, and they exude
deep emotions, usually rather melancholy, about human
indignities and sufferings.

Rebellion and Decline

In the last years of Hsüan-tsung's reign T'ang plummeted
into a decline that could never be reversed. The turning point
was 745, when the aging emperor became infatuated with a
deliciously plump young concubine, Lady Yang. Her relatives quickly won the prime ministership and other high
offices, and the emperor lost interest in government, doing
nothing to stop the deterioration of the equal-fields system
and the military. In 750 an aboriginal chieftain in Yunnan
rebelled and established a large southwestern kingdom called
Nan Chao. In 751 a T'ang army sent to punish him was
destroyed. In the same year T'ang forces on the far western
frontier were badly beaten in a famous battle at the Talas
River near Samarkand by Turks in league with Arabs, whose

militant expansion of Islam was then at high tide. Finally, in 755, one of Lady Yang's favorites, a Turk named An Lu-shan, who had been given supreme command over the strongest armies in China Proper, rose in rebellion. T'ang's demoralized western armies were ordered home and abandoned Chinese Turkestan to Moslem dominance.

The An Lu-shan rebellion forced Hsüan-tsung and his palace entourage to flee south from Ch'ang-an across the mountains into Szechwan. En route, Lady Yang was denounced and strangled, and Hsüan-tsung in grief and humiliation abdicated his shaky throne to a son. Rebels and loyalists fought on until 763, ravaging large areas of China. A Turkic group known as the Uighurs, who had taken command in Mongolia in 744, and even Arabs from Central Asia gave the loyalists such help that when peace was finally restored the T'ang court found itself virtually a vassal of the Uighur khan. Moreover, circuit intendants had been given such free rein to cope with the rebels that, as in Later Han, they had made themselves almost autonomous regional warlords over whom the central government had little control.

T'ang China now entered a kind of prolonged twilight. Although a facade of normalcy persisted, the central government not only had greatly restricted political authority, but was fiscally dependent in large part, first, on a revived and highly profitable salt monopoly and, later, on payments from regional authorities that had to be negotiated. Under a new so-called two-tax system, taxes were levied primarily on land rather than on persons. This was a notable retreat from the old idea that the state was responsible for rectifying inequities in land distribution. It was in fact an unavoidable recognition of free private ownership, with all its pitfalls for the poor peasant.

Most significantly, perhaps, the An Lu-shan rebellion began the breakdown of the old aristocracy of great-family shih. Military adventurers came to the forefront during the rebellion, and afterward the old social distinctions were blurred. Society became more open, and broadly recruited civil officials vied for influence in the central government with aliens and spies of regional warlords. As in other times of factional struggles, emperors gave increased authority to palace eunuchs, until they finally came to command the strongest armies at the capital and could manipulate the court as they wished. Two emperors were assassinated by eunuchs, and after 820 most emperors were installed by, and were puppets of, eunuch cliques.

Late T'ang Culture

In the long T'ang twilight after the great eighth-century rebellion, Chinese culture continued to flourish and change. Another poet of immense popularity appeared—Po Chü-i (772–846), a prodigy who passed the government's doctoral examination at the age of eighteen, had a distinguished official career, and produced some of China's best-loved poems, including a long and lugubrious ballad about the tragic love affair of Hsüan-tsung and Lady Yang. In prose there was at last a strong reaction against the stilted "parallel prose" style that dominated formal writings, led by a litterateur-official named Han Yü (786–824). He advocated and practiced an "old-style prose" (*ku-wen*), reviving the simple, uncluttered, forceful style of antiquity. It should be noted, though, that this was not a movement toward writing in the vernacular; it was just the reverse. Whether in "parallel prose" or "old-style prose," Chinese as written by the educated elite remained far different from Chinese as it was spoken.

Fiction. Because of the vigor and flexibility of ku-wen, its revival is credited with making possible, during the late T'ang years, the development of Chinese fiction from its earlier, very anecdotal forms into full short stories or novellas, which were written in profusion and collected in anthologies. Although supernatural elements remain strong in them, they are most notable for their realistic characterizations and their glimpses into everyday life among the T'ang urban class, especially in Ch'ang-an.

The Buddhist decline. Buddhism now passed its peak of development and influence in China. As Confucian-educated civil officials became more influential, and as the central government's fiscal difficulties grew, the Buddhist establishment became more vulnerable to attack because of its accumulated wealth and privileges. From 841 to 845 the government imposed the severest suppression in the history of Chinese Buddhism. The court had Buddhist institutions all over the country destroyed, exempting only four temples each in Ch'ang-an and Loyang and only one in each of the empire's other prefectures from the order. It was reported that 4,600 monasteries and 40,000 temples and shrines were wiped out; 260,500 monks and nuns were returned to the laity; and millions of acres of tax-exempt farmland were confiscated and returned to the tax registers. The result was not the extinction of Chinese Buddhism, by any means, but a great weakening of its institutional influence.

At the same time, Buddhism was declining as an intellectual force, and it was being attacked on philosophical grounds by China's civil officials, who were breathing new intellectual life into Confucianism. In the forefront was the prose stylist Han Yü, who wrote some strongly polemical essays denouncing Buddhism and reasserting the primacy of Confucianism.

Material culture. Everyday life had changed markedly by late T'ang times, as measured against Han. The Chinese now sat at tables on chairs instead of squatting on mats. They had learned to use coal as fuel, centuries earlier than Europeans. They used windmills and waterwheels to power irrigation systems. On the narrow trails of the south they pushed wheelbarrows, sometimes with the help of small sails, and rode in sedan-chairs. New fruits and spices had been introduced with the increasing incorporation of the south and increasing contacts with Southeast Asia and Central Asia. In

T'ang times tea became the national drink, in part because Buddhists championed it, as European churchmen did much later, in a temperance campaign against the old intoxicants distilled from grain or fruit. Paper, though invented in Han times, came into wide use only in subsequent years. By the T'ang era, paper had made possible a significant expansion of literacy, education, and manuscript libraries. Before the end of the dynasty woodblock printing had been invented, though the full impact of this development was not to be felt until later.

The End of T'ang

The T'ang twilight began to fade out in another great rebellion, lasting from 875 to 884. Beginning as a popular uprising in drought-stricken Honan, it quickly spread through eastern, central, and southern China under the leadership of a disgruntled salt merchant named Huang Ch'ao. In 879, when the rebels took Canton, they slaughtered thousands of foreign merchants there—Moslems, Jews, Christians, and Manichaeans. Huang then moved northward and in 881 captured Ch'ang-an. As at the time of the An Lu-shan rebellion, the T'ang court fled into Szechwan. When T'ang loyalists, with great help from Turkic allies, at last suppressed the rebellion, the empire was divided among rival warlords beyond hope of reunification. The dynasty survived for a few years more but ruled in name only. In 907, the last T'ang emperor was forced to abdicate by the foremost warlord of North China, a onetime follower of Huang Ch'ao.

The Five Dynasties and the Ten Kingdoms

For the next two generations, from 907 to 960, China endured another transitional age of political disunion. The end of T'ang prompted regional warlords to establish their own dynastic states. Those in the south are known as the Ten Kingdoms; they enjoyed relative peace, stability, and prosperity. North China was soon reconsolidated, but so shakily that five dynasties rapidly succeeded one another in the space of a half century.

Meantime a new nomad empire had emerged in Manchuria and eastern Mongolia under the leadership of a proto-Mongol people called the Ch'i-tan (Khitan). In 916 the Ch'i-tan khan declared himself emperor in Chinese fashion, calling his dynasty Liao. Ch'i-tan pressures contributed to the instability of North China. In the 930's the Chinese ceded the whole Peking region to Liao and began sending the khan annual tribute of coins and silk. In 946–47 the Ch'i-tan invaded and undertook to rule all North China directly, but they soon realized their inability to do so permanently and withdrew from the Yellow River area, content to be recognized as overlords by the North Chinese.

So dwindled away the heritage of T'ang's greatness—in regional fragmentation and partial subjugation to aliens.

THE LATER EMPIRE

960 - 1850

During the Five Dynasties era a new style of governance gradually evolved in the north, and in 960 a dynasty emerged that would once more unify China and usher in a period of unity, centralization, prosperity, and cultural flowering. China now was greatly constricted, however, not even incorporating all of what we have called China Proper. It was threatened by a series of new nomad powers to the north, and it experienced another cycle from unity to disunity to unity, overlaid with cycles of alien invasions and conquests. This later imperial age is treated here in the following subdivisions:

1. Sung, established in 960, which unified most of China Proper and made peace with the Ch'i-tan but collapsed in 1126 under attack by new northern nomads, the Jurchen. Driven into the south, Sung was not finally extinguished until 1279, when it was overrun by the classical nomad power of world history, the Mongols proper.

2. The great age of nomadism, which culminated, after Sung China had been encroached on successively by the Ch'i-tan Liao and the Jurchen Chin states, in the overlordship of the Mongols of Chingis (Genghis) and Kubilai Khan, who built the most extensive land empire ever known, and ruled all China as one of its provinces in the Yüan dynasty.

3. Ming, a dynasty under which the Chinese recovered control of their national destiny in 1368, and which conservatively established the institutional foundations for the modern Chinese state.

4. Ch'ing, the last of China's imperial dynasties, a Manchu dynasty that took over the Ming establishment in 1644. Under strong Manchu leaders, China flourished increasingly until pressures from the expanding West, combined with accumulated domestic discontents, undermined its stability and affluence in the nineteenth century.

Superficially, the dominant historic theme of this millennium is China's vain struggle to defend itself, first, against the northern nomads who were its traditional enemies and, in the end, against modern Western imperialists and domestic rebels. More fundamentally, however, China experienced dramatic domestic changes. The old aristocracy lost its dominance to a new bureaucratic elite of scholar-officials. Emperors became more autocratic than before. The population expanded until it finally exhausted the resources for its support. Urbanism and mercantilism became more prominent aspects of Chinese life. Buddhism lost its intellectual primacy to a dynamic Neo-Confucianism that stabilized into an orthodox ideology supporting the status quo. New forms of literature and art, new crops, and new manufactures appeared. All these changes gave China of late imperial times a distinctively different style from that of the early empire.

Sung

The dynasties that successively governed North China from 907 to 960, dreaming of restoring the T'ang empire, had whittled away at the powers of regional governors in the north and had begun the development of palace armies that could support a powerful central government. Concentrating on this domestic problem, they had allowed the Ch'i-tan to win ascendancy along the northern frontier and a confederation of Tibetan tribes called Tanguts to dominate the northwestern passageway to Central Asia. The consolidation of the north was proceeding successfully when a boy emperor succeeded to the throne of the dynasty called Later Chou.

Fearful of the consequences of weak leadership, the palace army mutinied in 960 and acclaimed its commander, Chao K'uang-yin, founder of a new dynasty, Sung.

The Founding

Sung T'ai-tsu (Grand Progenitor, Chao's posthumous designation; r. 960–76) prudently continued with the consolidation of the north. In one of the most remarkable coups of Chinese history, he first persuaded his own chief military supporters to yield their commands in return for generous retirement pensions, thus forestalling any possibility of a successful mutiny against himself. Then, gradually and tactfully, he replaced militaristic regional governors of the old order with civil officials delegated from his new court. He transferred the best personnel of the regional armies to the palace army, and that army he carefully kept under his personal command.

T'ai-tsu further helped ensure his supremacy by expanding the examination-recruitment system of the civil service and entrusting government at all levels to its scholar-officials. Through them, he attained centralized control over all revenues down to the county level. Because the new bureaucrats characteristically had no territorial power bases of their own but owed their status entirely to imperial favor, the system T'ai-tsu installed provided for a concentration of power in the throne beyond anything attained by earlier dynasties. From his time on, Chinese emperors were no longer *primus inter pares*, first among equals in an elite of powerful families. They were supreme autocrats, separated from their officials and subjects by so awesome a social gap that regicides and usurpations, formerly commonplace, now became extreme rarities (except in alien dynasties). Chinese dynasties were stabler, more centralized, and less vulnerable to domestic uprisings than before.

T'ai-tsu knew better than to abuse his expanding powers.

He encouraged his officials to be imaginative and bold, and in general followed an admirable policy of seeking and heeding their counsel. He also used officials very flexibly, assigning competent people wherever they were most needed, whatever their formal titles and ranks. Moreover, instead of repeating the Han and T'ang mistake of appointing circuit intendants who could become de facto regional governors, he sent out functionally differentiated intendants in a maze of overlapping circuits—for general administration, tax collection, judicial administration, military control, and so on—so that no one man had overall authority over any group of prefectures. From his modest capital built at Kaifeng in the center of the North China plain, T'ai-tsu established so strong a precedent of close collaboration with his civil service establishment that the whole Sung era was freer of abuses by palace women and eunuchs than any other major era of Chinese history. All these policies were perpetuated by T'ai-tsu's younger brother, who succeeded him as T'ai-tsung (r. 976–97).

Sung's Limited Expansion

While T'ai-tsu was in the process of establishing his administration and its guiding principles, he had also been systematically absorbing regional kingdoms in the south. Sung campaigns between 963 and 975 reduced them one after another except Wu-Yüeh in modern Chekiang, the southwestern aboriginal state called Nan Chao, which retained its independence throughout Sung times, and Vietnam, which on the collapse of T'ang had begun its development as an independent state. In 978 his brother T'ai-tsung accepted the surrender of Wu-Yüeh, and the following year he destroyed a Ch'i-tan puppet state in Shansi. Thus the traditional Chinese homeland was reunified except for Nan Chao and Vietnam, the far northwest (where the Tanguts had proclaimed a Chinese-style state of their own, called Hsi

Hsia), and the tier of 16 northeastern prefectures that Liao controlled. Vietnam and Hsi Hsia accepted nominal status as vassals.

The Sung expansion went no farther. T'ai-tsung twice campaigned northward in attempts to recover the Liao-dominated prefectures but was beaten off. In 1004 Liao sent a military probe toward Kaifeng but was checked. Thereupon the Sung and Liao rulers made a peace agreement, in accord with which Liao kept the northern prefectures, and Sung sent Liao silver and silk as "brotherly gifts" annually. Decades later Liao demanded and got increased annual tribute, but it kept the peace with Sung for more than a century. Hsi Hsia, however, provoked an inconclusive war in the northwest in the 1040's. Peace was arranged when Sung agreed to give Hsi Hsia annual tribute, too. When Hsi Hsia continued its harassments, Sung mounted punitive campaigns against it in 1069 and in 1081–82; both were ineffective.

In the eleventh century Sung was a very populous and wealthy state. The population swelled beyond the T'ang peak to some 100,000,000 by 1100. New fast-growing, drought-resistant rices were introduced, and agricultural production boomed. Craft industries multiplied and expanded. Freed from the discriminatory restraints of the early empire, mercantile enterprises of all sorts thrived. A genuinely national urban class developed for the first time in Chinese history. Government revenues increased in multiples of the T'ang totals; those from the monopolies of salt, tea, liquor, alum, and certain imported spices and luxury goods rose from 11,000,000 strings of coins in 997 to 50,000,000 strings in 1076. The economy became so monetized that there was a chronic shortage of copper for coinage, and the world's first paper money began circulating. In most respects China had reached a level of economic development not achieved by any European nation until the eighteenth century at the earliest. National iron production soared to an annual total of 125,000 tons—a sixfold per capita increase since the ninth century, and a level not attained anywhere in Europe until the Industrial Revolution.

Sung's soldiers were regularly equipped with iron and even steel arms and armor, and with a variety of incendiary weapons using gunpowder. By the middle of the eleventh century the regular, professional standing army was 1,250,-000 strong. Why, then, did Sung China not fight more zealously and effectively to restore the empire to its Han and T'ang extent? The simplest answer seems to be that, with civil officials replacing the old aristocracy, China was losing its will to fight. In the eleventh century the Chinese elite simply had more interesting and challenging, and in its view more important, things to attend to. Buying peace was worth the price.

Confucian Reformism

The invention of printing in the T'ang period, and the new prestige and affluence of the examination-recruited civil service, led to a great broadening of literacy and bookishness in the early Sung centuries. The early empire's aristocrats, for all their bookishness, were primarily horsemen whose real interests lay in hunting, falconry, polo, and war. The new bureaucratic elite that reached maturity in Sung times was preeminently a learned class, disdainful of war as of other nonintellectual pursuits. Although these new leaders remained interested in Buddhism and Taoism, their education directed them to the ancient classics associated with Confucianism, especially such works as the *Classic of Changes* and the *Chou Rituals*. There they found hints of answers to the problems for which Chinese had long thought Buddhism provided the only solutions, and also for the problems created by Buddhist prominence. In the eleventh century the excitement of rediscovering the classics produced an array of brilliant intellectuals unequaled in number in any other period of Chinese history, and they dominated political and social as well as philosophical life.

In the eleventh century the Confucian philosophical revival centered on building a new cosmology on the basis of the *Classic of Changes,* influenced in large part by Taoist traditions, in a movement that eventually undermined the pessimistic world view of the Buddhists. The new philosophy matured only in Southern Sung times and will be discussed below.

The most prominent aspect of the new intellectualism in the eleventh century was social reformism, which centered on a revival in the family and the secular community of a sense of mutual responsibility. The old Ch'in-Han aversion to extended families had gradually disappeared. It was now state dogma that the more successfully several generations could be kept together in one household, the stabler society would be. The noted scholar-official Fan Chung-yen (989–1052) led in organizing related families of a region into a corporate clan for the common welfare—to maintain clan schools and temples, to support clan widows, to provide loans to needy clan members, and in general to foster clan interests of every sort. Fan and others arranged for parcels of land to be entailed as clan properties in perpetuity to provide rental income for clan enterprises, and they drew up "clan instructions" that set forth standards for personal conduct and principles for the management of clan affairs. In some measure clans replaced the old great families as locally powerful groups that could protect individuals and nuclear families against outlawry and the abuses of local officials; and clan leaders came to be looked to by government authorities as guarantors of local stability and leaders in desirable community projects.

The new leaders also began promoting broader cooperation and mutual help by drawing up "community compacts," in which village families organized themselves for settling interfamily disputes, establishing community schools, fostering economic development projects such as irrigation systems, and maintaining local order—thus providing for a measure of local self-government, which was not merely tolerated but encouraged by the dynastic government.

Wang An-shih. On a larger scale officials now had unsurpassed opportunities to strive for governmental ideals rooted in such classics as the *Chou Rituals.* Fan Chung-yen established the credo of all Confucian ministers of the late imperial age by proclaiming that "the true scholar should be the first to become anxious about the world's troubles and the last to enjoy its happiness," and in 1043–44 he and a group of idealistic supporters led the central government in a ten-point reform program focusing mainly on personnel recruitment and local administration. Soon a new program was launched by the chief councilor Wang An-shih (1021-86), one of the most noted poets and classical commentators of the time and China's most ambitious and controversial reformer since Wang Mang 1,000 years earlier.

Wang An-shih's 15-point program of New Laws, promulgated between 1069 and 1073, was an almost Legalistic assertion of the state's responsibility for manipulating and reshaping society. The program principally involved these reforms:

1. Creating a Finance Planning Commission to coordinate all aspects of government, civil and military, administrative and censorial. With Wang as its leader, this body superseded the old Council of State and set a precedent for a strong prime ministership, which characterized government through the rest of the Sung period.

2. Expanding the system of state-supported local schools, emphasizing utilitarian training in such specialties as agronomy and medicine, and doing away with the T'ang variety of recruitment examinations, which all stressed memorization, in favor of a single *chin-shih,* or doctoral, examination that emphasized writing skill and the application of classical principles and historical precedents to current governmental problems.

3. Reducing the size and cost of the professional standing

army, and theoretically increasing China's military effectiveness, by replacing the professionals with better motivated
and well-trained militiamen, who, on short-term rotational
assignments, could maintain the national defenses.

4. Providing seed loans to peasants at relatively low interest rates to prevent their being foreclosed by usurious
moneylenders among the large landowning class.

5. Imposing new taxes on merchant guilds instead of the
traditional semi-confiscatory requisitions of goods needed by
the state, and setting up state warehouses that were something like wholesale pawnshops or resale shops dealing in
craft and industrial goods of every sort.

Wang An-shih's reforms were hotly contested by conservative officials, partly because of Wang's high-handed methods
in initiating them, partly because of their costly and bungled
implementation, and partly because they adversely affected
the official class itself, which was now the new privileged
landowning elite. The conservatives prevailed after a short
time and terminated the most unworkable of Wang's programs, such as his military reforms. But Wang's supporters
returned to power under the weak emperor Hui-tsung (r.
1100–1125); they then ousted anti-Wang officials as a trea-
sonable clique, and even ordered the destruction of some of
their writings.

Early Sung Literature and Art

The eleventh-century officials, when out of office or in
what must have been their abundant leisure while in office,
devoted themselves assiduously to classical scholarship, historical research, and writing the traditional forms of literary
prose and poetry—establishing a genteel life-style that was to
prevail among officials until the end of the imperial epoch.
Printing made it possible for their writings to be circulated
widely and preserved in abundance. It became common for
men of any distinction to publish their collected writings, or
for friends or descendants to do so.

Ku-wen literature. The ultimate triumph of the dynamic "old-style prose" championed by Han Yü in the ninth century was not achieved until the eleventh century, and it was then brought about almost single-handedly and against much traditionalist opposition by one of the all-around intellectual giants of Chinese history, Ou-yang Hsiu (1007–72). His protégés included men of such widely divergent personalities and views as the reformers Fan Chung-yen and Wang An-shih and several leaders in the opposition to Wang, especially Su Shih (or Su Tung-p'o, 1037–1101). Ou-yang's memorials and essays in old-style prose were of such unexcelled lucidity and power that many scholar-officials, notably including Wang and Su, emulated the style, with the result that by the time of Ou-yang's death it was firmly established as the standard for belles-lettres.

Among many other things Ou-yang Hsiu was co-author of a T'ang history and sole author of a history of the Five Dynasties era. But the premier historian of the eleventh century—and the greatest historian of the whole late imperial age—was Ssu-ma Kuang (1019–86), who happened also to be the leading political opponent of Wang An-shih. Sent into an enforced retirement of 15 years by Wang's supporters, he put the time to use to write a compendious, integrated narrative chronicle of Chinese history from 404 B.C. to A.D. 960: the *Comprehensive Mirror for Aid in Governance (Tzu-chih t'ung-chien)*. This work, which led to many subsequent abbreviated versions and sequels, established a new genre of historical writing, set new standards for the breadth of sources used, and introduced a methodology noted for remarkable sophistication and objectivity.

Poetry. Of the many noteworthy poets who flourished in early Sung times, the most versatile and renowned was Ou-yang Hsiu's protégé and Ssu-ma Kuang's political aide Su Shih. Perhaps the outstanding all-around aesthete of the entire Chinese tradition, Su was a recognized connoisseur of inks, wines, and cookery; an engineer who supervised water-control projects that made Hangchow with its West Lake one of the beauty spots of China; a practitioner of Taoist yoga and alchemy; and a brilliant writer of all forms of belles-lettres, especially poetry. He was most of all a master of the song-form called tz'u. The irregularities and complexities of meter and rhyme that characterize this form are suggested in the following translation of one of Su's two-stanza works:

Returning at Night to Lin-kao

Drinking at night on East Slope, I sober up only to get drunk again,
And it must be nearly the third watch when I return.
The houseboy's snores are thunderous roars.
I bang on the gates, but no one waits.
So I lean on my staff and listen to the river churn.

I heave long sighs that my life is not my own.
When will I get free from these trifling troubles!
Late in the night the wind grows calm, the waves become bubbles.
In a small boat I could break away from here with ease
And give my remaining life to the rivers and seas!

Fiction and drama. Sung intellectuals were not dedicated to writing fiction of the sort that became popular in late T'ang, but vernacular fiction, both short and long, was being developed in oral form by professional storytellers who entertained the crowds in Sung's growing urban centers. There were also the crude beginnings of a popular dramatic tradition, in two styles. One was a vaudeville-like variety show (*tsa-chü*) that was performed in theaters, of which eleventh-century Kaifeng had more than 50. The other was a category of romantic, sad narrations interspersed with erotic songs that were performed by courtesans in tea-houses and better-class brothels in the cities.

The arts. Hard-glazed porcelain wares now came to be fully developed, and a variety of wares were produced in different localities: very thin eggshell wares in white with a faint blue-green tint, called Ju; glossy blue-gray wares called

Kuan; Ting wares with pure white bodies, often incised with floral designs, and sumptuously overcoated in a creamy glaze running into teardrop clusters; and many others. Sung wares generally were monochromes and are renowned for their elegantly, classically simple shapes as cups, bowls, vases, and the like. The export of Chinese porcelains throughout Asia and across the Indian Ocean to the Mediterranean world contributed importantly to Sung's foreign trade.

Painting in Sung times was developing in two directions. On one hand, Sung emperors established a painting academy at court, where professionals devoted themselves to rather realistic watercolors including not only formal portraits, but also pictures of birds, flowers, and landscapes, all highly decorative. The emperor Hui-tsung was himself a master and connoisseur of this style and patronized a large corps of court painters. An annotated catalogue of his imperial collection listed 6,396 paintings by 231 artists. On the other hand, the new class of scholar-officials was producing great amateur painters as well as litterateurs. They characteristically painted monochromes in different shadings of black ink, and especially landscapes done in a moodily impressionistic style rather than realistically. All schools of painters particularly esteemed calligraphy, in which the perfection of brushwork is all-important. Su Shih was one of the most famous calligraphers of his time, and also a sensitive painter of greatly admired bamboo stalks.

Transition to the South

Wang An-shih's principal purpose had been to strengthen the state and its officialdom. His legacy, however, was a bankrupt treasury and a bureaucracy torn by vindictive partisanship. Under Hui-tsung in the early 1100's the Sung state drifted. Meantime, a new nomad power, the proto-Manchu people called Jurchen, had organized in Manchuria beyond the Liao empire. In 1115 the Jurchen chief proclaimed himself emperor of a dynasty called Chin. The Sung

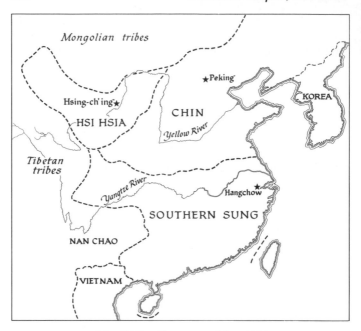

Map 5. The Chinese world, c. 1150

court, which for some time had been receiving seaborne diplomatic missions from the Jurchen, readily made a treaty with Chin to join in crushing Liao between them. In 1125, after a seven-year war, this goal was achieved with Chin's capture of the last Liao emperor. But then the Chin-Sung alliance collapsed, and Chin armies brought Kaifeng under siege.

It is to Sung's credit that Kaifeng was defended with vigor. By this time Chinese soldiers were using firebombs and tank-like carts sheathed in iron armor, and they fought well. The government surrendered only when the city ran out of supplies and its residents were reduced to cannibalism. The Jurchen then appointed a puppet governor and withdrew, but they returned and sacked the city when he failed to deliver an impossible indemnity that Chin required. Thus in 1127 Sung lost its base in North China. Hui-tsung and the son to whom he had already abdicated were carried off into captivity, along with 3,000 members of the Sung court. Chin set up its capital at Peking, and Jurchen armies pressed on southward.

Sung patriots now established another son of Hui-tsung as successor emperor at Nanking, and irregular resistance forces arose throughout central China in his defense. For more than a decade Chinese and Jurchen fought for supremacy in the Yangtze River valley. Finally, in 1138, the new ruler, Kao-tsung (r. 1127–62), was stably settled in a new capital, Hangchow, on the coast south of the Yangtze, and Sung generals were winning some victories over the Jurchen. In 1142 peace was negotiated. Sung retained control of the Yangtze River drainage area but ceded North China to Chin. It accepted formal status as a vassal of Chin and agreed to pay Chin annual tribute in silver and silk.

During the prolonged fighting, the Sung government became seriously divided. One group wanted peace. Another wanted to continue the war in the hope of recovering the north. The peace of 1142 seems to have been a realistic settlement of a military stalemate. But the Sung chief councilor who negotiated it, Ch'in Kuei (1090–1155), was forever after derided as a traitorous appeaser; and the most successful Sung general, Yüeh Fei (1103–41), became the symbol of heroic, tragic patriotism for all later generations of Chinese. Yüeh was imprisoned for obstinately objecting to the peace negotiations, and was murdered in prison. For the rest of the Southern Sung era, the officialdom was regularly upset by partisan antagonisms rooted in the transitional era's policy differences. But there was no new large-scale war with Chin. Inconclusive border fighting between Chinese and Jurchen flared up in 1161, 1165, and 1206, and the original peace treaty was twice renegotiated, first reducing and later increasing Sung's tribute payments.

The loss of North China to aliens and the need to maintain a strong defense line north of the Yangtze did not prevent the continued flourishing of Chinese life and culture in the south, which, with the exception of Nan Chao's domain in the southwest, was now wholly occupied by Chinese and intensively developed. Whether measured per acre or per capita, agricultural production steadily increased. Commerce, both domestic and foreign, thrived even more, until commercial taxes became a more substantial proportion of the government's total revenue than at any other time in all of China's imperial history.

The notable urbanizing trend of the Northern Sung era now accelerated, and for once in its history China seemed almost as much a nation of shopkeepers as one of farmers. Hangchow became the most populous metropolis the world had ever known, with a resident population of some 2,000,-000 within its walls and another 2,000,000 in its immediate environs. The famous Venetian traveler Marco Polo, who visited Hangchow soon after its prime, was overawed by its size, its varied commerce, its lively social life, and its numerous amusement districts, whose theaters often had multiple tiers of balconies. Another European visitor reported that the residents of the congested market quarters around any one of the 13 gates in Hangchow's city wall exceeded the total population of Venice; and of Ch'üan-chou in Fukien, Southern Sung's principal port, Polo reported that more ships lay at anchor in its harbor on any one day than docked at Venice or Genoa in a whole year. All such reports were considered outrageous lies in Europe, whose greatest cities at that time had at most 50,000 residents. It was equally impossible for contemporary Europeans to believe that the Chinese government was printing and circulating paper money. But Southern Sung issued billions of cash equivalents in paper not backed by cash reserves, causing a steady inflation that could not be checked.

Neo-Confucianism

In Southern Sung times the philosophical ferment of the eleventh century culminated in the systematic formulation of what Westerners call Neo-Confucianism. To the Chinese of the time the movement was known as "the study of the Way" (*Tao-hsüeh*), and it included a wide spectrum of thinkers who engaged in public debates, carried on voluminous correspondence with each other, and established private academies where they taught large groups of followers. Buddhism and Taoism were by no means dead; Ch'an Buddhist intellectuals were perhaps only now at their peak of influence, respected and befriended even by zealous Confucians. The reformist activism of Northern Sung also persisted among materialistic, utilitarian advocates of practical statecraft, somewhat reminiscent of ancient Legalist rationalism. Traditional, conservative Confucian moralists remained influential, too—so much so that the Sung state sometimes denounced all of the new Tao-hsüeh teachings as subversive, and banned them.

The dominant strain of thought in these times, evolving out of the cosmological speculations of Northern Sung, was fully developed and systematically articulated by the scholar-official Chu Hsi (1130–1200), whose doctrines were fundamental to all subsequent intellectual development in China and also in Vietnam, Korea, and Japan. Chu Hsi-ism postulates a dualistic universe consisting of abstract principles (*li*) in dynamic combination with matter, stuff, or ether (*ch'i*). The summation of all principles is the Supreme Ultimate (*t'ai-chi*), an impersonal cosmic force corresponding to the naturalistic conception of Tao in the Taoist tradition. Its principles combine with matter in a process motivated by the generative interaction of yang and yin forces, to produce all individual things including human beings. Ch'i thus contributes the physical substance of man, including physical appetites such as lust, whereas li contributes the form or nature of man-ness, which differentiates men as a category from all other beings and things, each of which is shaped by its different li. Men differ from one another because of the particular combinations of li with ch'i that result from the particular circumstances of each birth.

According to Chu Hsi, the goal of every man is or should be to become a sage—that is, to fulfill the potentiality of his li, the principle of humanness, and associate himself ever more intimately with the Supreme Ultimate. Man can do this by developing a strong sense of sincerity or earnestness and by devoting himself to "the cultivation of the self" through "the investigation of things"—terms drawn from a minor classic of late Chou times. The result sought is neither salvation Buddhist-style nor immortality Taoist-style, but becoming a man in the fullest, best, most gratifying sense, much as Confucius had advocated.

Chu Hsi-ism has parallels with Platonic thought, and "the investigation of things" that it advocates unquestionably has similarities with the modern scientific spirit. However, the "things" that Chu Hsi and his followers principally emphasized were not natural laws, but the ethical virtues traditionally espoused by Confucianism—filial piety, loyalty, humankindness, and the like, each of which exists as an abstract principle in Chu Hsi's view. Consequently, Chu Hsi-ism became a bookish, conservative search for classical precepts and historical precedents that best expressed such virtues. Chu Hsi annotated the classics with this goal in mind and in the same spirit compiled a moralistic abbreviation of Ssu-ma Kuang's great historical compendium, the *Comprehensive Mirror for Aid in Governance.* His conservatism, and especially his emphasis on loyalty, naturally appealed to the autocratic rulers of the late empire. By the end of Sung in 1279, it was common for his interpretations of the classics and history to be used as a standard in the civil service recruit-

ment examinations, and in all later dynasties they were
mandatory.

Late Sung Literature and Art

Literature. Southern Sung litterateurs were as prolific as
their society was affluent. Two new forms of scholarly prose
were now added to the heritage. One was "pen jottings" (*sui-
pi* or *pi-chi*), a kind of scholar's notebook containing hundreds
or thousands of short pieces ranging from serious historical or
classical research notes to trivia of every sort, which make
delightful browsing and are excellent sources for social
history. Among the most renowned of these is one of the
earliest, *Jottings from the Leisure Studio (Jung-chai sui-pi)*, by
Hung Mai (1123–1202). The other newly prominent form was
the local history or gazetteer, pioneered long before. Early in
Southern Sung, Meng Yüan-lao produced a valuable descriptive memoir on the lost capital, Kaifeng; this was followed by
a similar description of Hangchow, produced as Southern
Sung was about to fall. More common were histories of
counties and prefectures, called gazetteers, in a composite
chronological-topical format resembling that long established for dynastic histories; almost 200 such gazetteers were
published in Southern Sung.

All scholar-officials were now poets, and memorable masters appeared in every generation. The most renowned
Southern Sung poet, Lu Yu (1125–1209), was one of the most
prolific versifiers of the Chinese heritage, churning out more
than 9,000 poems. Like his contemporaries, he wrote occasional poems marking the changing events and moods of his
everyday life and poems describing the ordinary scenes and
episodes of life in general, of which he was a fascinated
observer. What especially distinguishes him is that he wrote
an abundance of passionately patriotic poems, a rarity in the
Chinese heritage. The most famous example is his last poem,
written on his deathbed:

For My Son

When dead and gone one finally knows the vanity of all things,
But I still regret that I won't see the realm reunited.
When the imperial armies recover the Central Plain to the north,
In the family devotions don't forget to let your father know.

The arts. Magnificent monochrome porcelain wares continued to be produced in Southern Sung, both for domestic use and increasingly for export. Porcelain produced in the south most notably included celadons from kilns in Chekiang and Kiangsi—wares with an off-white body thickly covered with a translucent greenish glaze. Another famed category of Southern Sung porcelain is a ware produced in Hangchow with a very dark body and a crackled greenish or yellowish glaze, the crackles sometimes being accentuated with red or black stain. The best Southern Sung wares, elegantly simple in form like their Northern Sung predecessors, have a delicately soft and subtle beauty that is appreciated around the world.

China's painting tradition now reached what most connoisseurs consider its finest peak in moodily impressionistic, highly selective monochrome landscapes evoking the mystic grandeur of nature. The greatest masters were the twelfth-century court painters Ma Yüan and Hsia Kuei, who both lived on and worked into the early 1200's. Another famous painting style of the time was a spontaneous, slapdash, vibrantly strong style developed by Ch'an masters in the great Hangchow monasteries. The two most famous Ch'an stylists were Mu-ch'i and Liang K'ai. They did highly abstract, impressionistic ink paintings of commonplace objects or outline sketches of Ch'an masters and other figures.

The Extinction of Sung

After the transitional period the Southern Sung court at Hangchow was characterized by weak emperors, domineering chief councilors, and wrangling, do-nothing careerists in the officialdom. Defense was maintained at ever increasing cost, so that state finances were always strained despite increasing production, commerce, and general affluence. Taxation became a very heavy burden, borne largely by the urban mercantile classes. Large landowners, who were the class best represented in the officialdom, continued their steady reduction of the poor peasantry to tenancy and serfdom. In the 1260's a chief councilor tried to impose limits on landowning and to confiscate surplus holdings from well-to-do families so as to reestablish independent peasants, but he succeeded only in alienating the rural elite and creating new waves of partisan wrangling at court.

By this time Sung was threatened anew from the north with the sudden rise of the Mongols proper as a united nomad power under Chingis Khan and his successors. The Mongols first attacked the far northern frontier of Chin in 1210, then captured Peking in 1215, and in 1227 destroyed Hsi Hsia in the northwest. In 1232, following the same foreign policy that had been adopted against Liao more than a century before, Sung allied itself with the Mongols to crush the remnants of Chin between them. By 1234 Chin had been destroyed, and Sung armies were gleefully reoccupying Kaifeng and Loyang on the Yellow River. However, instead of recovering North China permanently, the Sung Chinese from 1235 on found themselves waging a desperate defensive war against the onrushing Mongols.

Sung's fortifications against Chin north of the Yangtze River proved to be the most formidable barrier the Mongols encountered in their sweeping campaigns across Eurasia. The fighting was heroic and ingenious on both sides. True explosive weapons—bomb-throwing catapults and bazooka-like bamboo tubes—came into use, first by the defenders and then by the attackers. The Mongols made good use of siege specialists brought in from the Near East. In 1273 they smashed the most critical Sung defenses and poured into the Yangtze River valley. Adapting swiftly to the naval fighting required by the southern terrain, they forced Hangchow to surrender without a fight in 1276 and exterminated the last organized Sung loyalist resistance in a sea battle off Canton in 1279. For the first time in history all of China Proper was now in the hands of alien overlords.

The Great Age of Nomadism

The Ch'i-tan, Jurchen, and Mongol tribesmen who successively threatened China from the north after the collapse of T'ang did not significantly differ in their patterns of origin and evolution from their counterparts of the early imperial age, the Hsiung-nu, Hsien-pi, and Turks. First appearing as forest hunters in eastern Siberia north of Korea, they moved down onto the steppes of northern Manchuria and Outer Mongolia, and there they gradually adopted the life-style of horse nomadism that was best suited to the terrain. Their tribal organization, herding economy, and battle tactics seem to have been essentially the same as those of the Hsiung-nu of Ch'in and Han times.

The nomadic groups never numbered more than a minute few compared with the sedentary, agrarian Chinese masses to the south; but to the extent that they could confederate under strong leaders and effectively exploit the advantages of their nomadic life-style, they were able to harass China and keep it on the defensive. Virtually living on horseback, and taking with them everywhere the herds that supplied them with meat, drink, wool clothing, and felt-tent housing, they could mobilize all their fighting forces on short notice at any point along the Chinese frontier. However carefully the Chinese might guard the Great Wall, the lack of extensive horse pasturages within China Proper and the consequent unskilled horsemanship of China's soldiery made it impossible for the traditional Chinese ever to match the striking power of the nomads at any point of attack. Moreover, the logistical difficulties of maintaining a large Chinese expedition northward made it almost impossible for the Chinese ever to pursue, catch, and destroy the elusive nomads on the open steppes.

Confronted with the great mobility of the nomads, China had to rely on the dogged defensive staying power of its land-bound peasantry, supported by heavier and more sophisticated weaponry than the nomads could manage. Thus it was the nature of things that, whereas the nomads could break through the Chinese frontier for looting raids at any particular point they chose to attack, the Chinese could normally stop the nomads at any particular point where they had time to organize for defense. Only to the extent that the nomads were willing and able to become Chinese—that is, settle down to an agrarian life on which they could build a stable government with revenues to support large infantry armies, siege weapons, and the like—only to that extent could the aliens control Chinese territory for long and make positive contributions to the mainstream development of Chinese civilization.

In this regard, the Ch'i-tan, the Jurchen, and the Mongols differed from such predecessors as the T'o-pa. They did not assimilate successfully with the Chinese. Consequently, although they controlled Peking and the northeast cumulatively for four centuries, all North China for two and a half centuries, and the whole of China Proper for a century, their impact on China was almost entirely negative. Chinese civilization survived in spite of them and developed in reaction against them; it was not positively transformed and advanced by them.

Liao

The proto-Mongol Ch'i-tan people whose Liao empire dominated Manchuria, eastern Mongolia, and northernmost China Proper from 916 to 1125 owed their nationhood to the chieftain Yeh-lü A-pao-chi (872–926). Taking control of the northeast upon the fall of T'ang, he recruited renegade

Chinese to serve in his administration and develop an agrarian supplement to the herding economy. However, the Ch'i-tan resisted Sinicization and retained their tribal ways more effectively than almost any other invaders of China. They organized their state in a strange dualistic structure, with a "north-facing" government to rule the Ch'i-tan by tribal customs and a "south-facing" government to rule the Chinese in a semblance of the T'ang manner. Educated Chinese were recruited in T'ang-style examinations, and Chinese farmers were drafted into infantry components of the Liao army. But the Chinese never had any real influence on the Ch'i-tan. Chinese were treated as an inferior caste; intermarriage was discouraged and sometimes forbidden. The Ch'i-tan showed only token interest in Chinese intellectual life. They developed no national literature of their own and remained primitive shamanists. They are remembered by the Chinese as barbarians to the end, revoltingly addicted to brutish punishments and human sacrifice.

Chin

The proto-Manchu Jurchen, whose Chin state dominated North China from 1127 to 1234, were less barbarous in Chinese eyes than either the Ch'i-tan or the Mongols. Although they were fierce cavalrymen feared by the Koreans as well as the Ch'i-tan in their early history, they were never fully committed to nomadism and admired Chinese civilization from the start, under their founding chieftain, Wan-yen A-ku-ta (1068–1123). Many Jurchen noblemen became serious students of Chinese literature, many classical Chinese works came to be translated into a Jurchen script, and the Chin government eventually became a reasonable approximation of T'ang's, with examination-recruited Chinese playing important roles in administration. Jurchen control of affairs was ensured by the clustering of Jurchen families in reservation-like military colonies throughout North China. But since the mature Chin empire's population was overwhelmingly Chinese and its economy was overwhelmingly agrarian, Sinicizing trends were natural and in large measure irresistible. Chin emperors nevertheless regularly fulminated against them and issued terrible threats against any adoption of Chinese names, dress, and customs among the Jurchen. The ablest of the later Chin rulers, Shih-tsung (r. 1161–89), tried especially to revive the militant Jurchen heritage, but in the end Chin's defenses against the rising Mongols to the north were heavily dependent on subject Ch'i-tan tribesmen. Many of the Jurchen who survived the eventual Mongol conquest seem to have been easily swallowed up in the general North China population, becoming Chinese without adding anything to Chineseness.

Yüan

In early Sung times the Mongolian-speaking peoples were scattered across the eastern Siberian plain in separate tribes or nations. One of the many tribes became the Mongols proper (*Meng-ku* in Chinese); another bore the name Tatar (*Ta-ta*), which outsiders eventually applied to all the non-Chinese of Mongolia, Manchuria, and Central Asia indiscriminately, even non-Mongolian speakers such as the Manchus.

In 1203 one tribal chief named Temuchin (1155–1227) assumed the title Chingis Khan (Universal Chief), and three years later he was elected grand khan in an assembly, or *kuriltai,* of all the Mongol leaders. There then began one of the most explosive series of conquests in world history. Proclaiming that there was no greater joy than massacring one's enemies, taking their horses and herds, and ravishing their women, Chingis left a trail of slaughter extending from Korea in the east to the Caspian Sea and the Don River in the west. His sons and grandsons pressed the Mongol campaigns on to Moscow and across Poland into Prussia, across Hungary and Austria almost to Trieste on the Adriatic, and across old Persia to the Mediterranean. To Christendom, Chingis was the long expected anti-Christ, the Scourge of God. To the

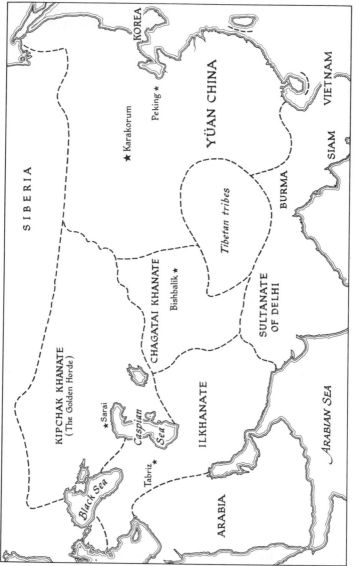

Map 6. The Mongol Empire, c. 1300

Chinese he was the most savage destroyer they had known. In his first sweep across the North China plain in 1212–13 he left 90-odd towns in rubble, and when he sacked Peking in 1215 the city burned for more than a month.

The mature Mongol empire included four khanates: (a) the Grand Khanate headquartered at Karakorum in Outer Mongolia, which incorporated Mongolia, Manchuria, Korea, and China, including the long independent states of Hsi Hsia and Nan Chao; (b) the Chagatai Khanate in Central Asia; (c) the Kipchak Khanate in southern Russia, popularly known as the Golden Horde; and (d) the Ilkhanate in the Near East. Under the early grand khans, who were elected in kuriltais at Karakorum, the vast empire was a strictly disciplined confederation, with the result that for the first time in history peaceful, untroubled travel from the Mediterranean world to East Asia was possible. European popes and kings sent envoys to the grand khans in the vain hope of allying Christendom and the Mongol empire in a combined holy war on Islam.

Kubilai Khan (r. 1260–94), a grandson of Chingis and the fifth grand khan, was the first northern alien to rule all China. Because he seized power at Karakorum by force without being elected in a kuriltai, he was often at war with the Mongols of Central Asia and exercised little authority beyond his own realm. This he changed into a Chinese-style empire, transferring his capital to Peking in 1264 and inaugurating a dynasty called Yüan in 1271, even before the extinction of Southern Sung. Succession was made hereditary rather than elective, a Chinese-style administration was established, and Yüan was proclaimed the rightful continuance of the heritage of Han and T'ang.

Unlike all previous rulers of China, Kubilai aggressively tried to extend his authority overseas. He sent out representatives to win recognition of his overlordship as far as Japan, Sumatra, Ceylon, and southern India. Twice, in 1274 and 1281, he tried to subjugate defiant Japan with massive naval assaults. The second effort combined fleets from Korea and the Yangtze delta into an armada of 4,500 ships and 150,000 men. Neither assault succeeded. Kubilai was somewhat more successful in 1292, when he dispatched a fleet to punish a recalcitrant potentate in Java. Nearer at hand, Tibet, Burma, Siam, Annam in northern Vietnam, and Champa in southern Vietnam all accepted status as tributary vassal states; and punitive campaigns against Burma and Annam in the 1280's, though not always resulting in military victories, brought reaffirmations of vassalage from rulers whose submissiveness had proved questionable.

Yüan government. At first the Mongols hardly knew what to do with China. They were essentially wreckers and looters, not builders or managers; and they had to be persuaded not to wipe out the Chinese and turn their lands into pastures. Even in the 1300's a Mongol chief councilor proposed, with some seriousness, that Chinese unrest should be dealt with by killing all Chinese with the five commonest surnames. If carried out, this massacre would have reduced the population perhaps by half. There was never any thought among the Mongols of their becoming Chinese, although they sometimes expediently performed the rituals and issued the edicts that were customary in the Chinese tradition. Their conquest led to an imperialistic military occupation of China, and the only problems they recognized were how best to keep the Chinese subdued and how best to exploit their resources.

In Kubilai's time it was resolved that the Chinese could be governed most satisfactorily under a governmental façade resembling their own traditional institutions, while being controlled in reality by Mongol garrisons stationed throughout the country. General administration was assigned to six T'ang-style ministries in the central government, coordinated by a unitary top-echelon agency, the Secretariat. Between the central government and the traditional prefectures and counties there evolved a complex network of administrative, surveillance, and military organs, including the forerunners of China's modern provinces. By law, only

Mongols could head any government agency, central or local. By preference, the Mongols delegated their routine administrative tasks to non-Chinese specialists from Central Asia, the Near East, and even Europe. Of necessity, however, educated Chinese had to be relied on in most low- and middle-rank posts. When the court was finally persuaded to reinstitute civil service recruitment examinations in 1315, quotas were established so that half of all the few chin-shih degrees awarded were won by Mongols and other non-Chinese, however poorly qualified by traditional standards.

Chinese humiliations. Developing a practice initiated by the Jurchen in North China, the Mongols classified all their subjects into rigid hereditary categories. One categorization was by occupation, with finely defined subgroups almost like castes, to each of which the government assigned appropriate state obligations, a mixture of taxes and services. At the bottom of this scale were many thousands of Chinese who were enslaved—probably more than at any other time in history—and were freely bought and sold at public slave markets. In addition, there was a simple four-class ethnic categorization that determined one's social status and political privileges. The four groups were, from top to bottom: (a) Mongols; (b) other non-Chinese; (c) North Chinese; and (d) South Chinese. South Chinese were the former subjects of Southern Sung. Accounting for 75–80 percent of the total Yüan population of some 60,000,000, the South Chinese in effect supported the rest of the population and were discriminated against in every conceivable fashion. They were generally labeled *Man-tzu*, a term traditionally used for aboriginal tribespeople, which could only be considered insulting by the Chinese.

All Chinese were forbidden by law to bear arms, to learn the Mongolian language, and to assemble in groups except for authorized religious and educational purposes. They had to scrape and bow, not only to the coarsest Mongol tribesman, but to all other non-Chinese. The Chinese especially resented having to humble themselves in the presence of priests of Tibetan Lamaism, perhaps the least intellectual and most shamanistic form of Buddhism. The Mongol rulers greatly admired lamas, installed them in all parts of China, and patronized them lavishly.

The Yüan economy. Centuries of alien invasions and occupations had so devastated and depopulated the north that South China was now China's breadbasket and marketing center, and the affluence of Southern Sung times persisted there, at least superficially, through the Yüan dynasty. The Mongols especially esteemed commerce and encouraged it both in China and abroad, in part by printing paper money at a faster rate even than Southern Sung, until finally there was runaway inflation. Whereas Southern Sung had maintained a substantial merchant marine, Yüan allowed Arab ships to carry China's trade throughout Southeast Asia and across the Indian Ocean. The government even contracted with favored merchants of the southeast coast to transport South China's tax rice around Shantung to the northern coast near Peking— some 3,500,000 bushels annually. Despite disastrous losses at sea, and even though the long-disused Grand Canal was reconstructed in the 1280's and 1290's, sea transport remained the major means of provisioning the officials and soldiers of the north to the end of the dynasty.

Government efforts to stimulate agriculture were not successful, in large part because of the Mongols' neglect of irrigation and other water-control projects that required substantial and continuing capital investments. The rulers, as at times in the past, could not restrain their counterproductive impulses to confiscate the best lands and grant them to nobles, to garrisons, and to monasteries. Some Mongol nobles seem to have converted large tracts of rice paddies in the south into resort-like parks and pasturages. By the early 1300's widespread starvation was regularly reported.

Two crops that were to become important in Chinese

agriculture were introduced at this time—sorghum in the north and cotton in the south.

Yüan culture. Traditionally hospitable to peaceful strangers, tolerant of different religions, and interested in trading profits, the Mongols encouraged foreigners of all sorts to swarm over China, and a cosmopolitan air prevailed resembling that of T'ang times. Not only Lamaism but also Islam, Manichaeism, Nestorian Christianity, and Roman Catholicism were introduced or reintroduced; and native Buddhist and Taoist monasticism and popular cults thrived. In 1280 the Franciscan friar John of Montecorvino (1246?–1328) was sent from Rome to be archbishop of Peking. When Marco Polo departed China in 1292 after 17 years of residence and travel there, he carried with him a request from Kubilai Khan for 100 more Catholic priests; and a few more Franciscans were sent to join Montecorvino and establish a bishopric at the Fukien port city Ch'üan-chou. Islam, spreading from Central Asia, gained a durable foothold along the western boundaries of China Proper.

Native intellectuals carried on the scholarly and literary traditions of the Sung period and absorbed themselves in the still-new and exciting Neo-Confucian doctrines. Deprived of the sociopolitical status and economic affluence they had gained in Sung times, they did not produce many outstanding works; many adopted a reclusive life-style. In painting the amateur, or literati, style was cultivated widely, but it turned away from the rather emotional impressionism of the great Southern Sung masters to a harsh, cool, intellectual expressionism, in which somewhat crude, primitive-seeming monochrome landscapes were thought to reveal, by the quality of their brushstrokes, the character of the painter. In ceramics Yüan was a transitional period between the elegant monochrome Sung tradition and the richly decorative polychrome tradition that would predominate in the later centuries.

Yüan is especially noteworthy as the great age of Chinese

theater. The early Sung variety shows and dramatic recita-
tions had continued to evolve in the north under the Jurchen
Chin dynasty, and by Mongol times they had coalesced into a
form that has ever since been considered China's classical
form of operatic drama, called *tsa-chü*. Tsa-chü are well
plotted, melodramatic four- or five-act plays combining
acting (ranging from mime to dancing and energetic acrobat-
ics), soliloquies and dialogue, and the singing of arias. They
are written in a mixture of the classical and vernacular forms
of language, include much bawdy buffoonery, and take their
plots primarily from long-familiar T'ang short stories or the
tales long told by professional storytellers. The Yüan conventions of costume, facial makeup, and artificial speech man-
nerisms on stage have endured into our own times, and
favorite portions of Yüan dramas have been standard items in
the repertoire of all Chinese theatrical troupes. Since tsa-chü
were considered vulgar by the educated elite until the end of
the imperial epoch, little is known about Yüan dramatists
beyond their names; but it is clear that several were geniuses.

The Mongol collapse. Kubilai had no distinguished successors on the Yüan throne. The succession ordinarily embroiled princes, nobles, empresses, and palace eunuchs in
intrigues that often erupted into mini-wars or other violence.
Three emperors were murdered. The authority of the throne
and the awesomeness of the dynasty declined substantially.
General ineptitude in government, factionalism among officials, military deterioration, economic distress, and a series of
earthquakes, floods, and famines at last reduced the Yüan
government to impotence in the 1340's. Chinese peasants
rose in desperate, uncoordinated revolts, and in the 1350's
the Mongols lost control of the Yangtze River valley to
fragmented rebel groups that struggled among themselves for
supremacy. In the 1360's, while Mongol factions warred on
each other in the north, a Chinese leader gradually consolidated the Yangtze drainage area. In 1368 he proclaimed a

new native dynasty based at Nanking, and as his armies marched northward the last Yüan emperor fled with his fellow Mongols back into the steppes of Mongolia.

Ming

The new native dynasty, Ming, was innovative and durable, lasting from 1368 to 1644. Under its rule, China was stable and affluent, and it dominated East Asia in the Han and T'ang fashion. The era is nevertheless not esteemed as a glorious, brilliant, splendid revival of the Chinese spirit. The centuries of nomadic batterings, invasions, and occupations had left their mark; and Ming China is perhaps best described, by and large, as a time of competent, prosperous, but somewhat subdued ordinariness.

The Founders

The founder of the Ming dynasty was the first commoner to rule over all China since the beginning of Han in 202 B.C. This was Chu Yüan-chang (b. 1328), known posthumously as T'ai-tsu (or by his era-name, Hung-wu; r. 1368–98). The son of itinerant tenant farmers of east central China, Chu was orphaned as a youth and accepted as a novice in a small Buddhist monastery. When hard times came he was sent out as a mendicant monk, and eventually he was drawn into a semireligious popular uprising. He soon became one of its most successful leaders. In 1356 he captured Nanking, and by the end of 1367 he had become a regional warlord dominating the Yangtze River valley from Szechwan to the Pacific. Proclaiming a new dynasty with its capital at Nanking in 1368, he sent armies to drive the Mongols out of North China and to extend his authority to the south coast. By the end of his 30-year reign, his armies had won secure control of modern China Proper and dominated the northern frontier regions from Hami, in modern Sinkiang province, through Inner Mongolia into northern Manchuria. In addition, vassalage in the traditional tributary system had been accepted by Korea, the oasis states of Chinese Turkestan, and the various countries of mainland Southeast Asia.

Early Ming militancy was continued by T'ai-tsu's son Ch'eng-tsu (or Yung-lo; r. 1402–24), who came to power by overthrowing his nephew, the designated heir apparent, in a three-year civil war. Concerned about the reorganizing Mongols in the north, Ch'eng-tsu personally led five military campaigns into Mongolia. He operated primarily out of his personal power base at Peking, and in 1421 he formally moved the Ming capital there from Nanking, having had the silted-up Grand Canal reengineered to carry annual grain shipments to the new capital and the northern frontier defense forces. Ch'eng-tsu was also not unmindful of problems and opportunities in the south. When northern Vietnam was troubled by succession problems, he intervened and incorporated it as a directly administered region of China, interrupting the independence it had enjoyed since the end of T'ang. Angered by Japanese raiders who had harassed the Yangtze delta throughout the fourteenth century, he bullied Japan into accepting tributary vassalage for the first time in history. He also dispatched large armadas, as the Mongols had, to collect tribute overseas in the south. His most famous admiral, a Moslem eunuch named Cheng Ho (1371–1433), led seven great naval expeditions between 1405 and 1433 that visited Java, Sumatra, Ceylon, southern India, Arabia, and the east coast of Africa, making China for the only time in history the unchallenged naval power in the South China Sea and the Indian Ocean.

Ming Autocracy

Both T'ai-tsu and Ch'eng-tsu inherited from their Mongol predecessors a highly autocratic style of governing. T'ai-tsu was especially despotic—and so capricious that his court officials are said to have bade their families farewell on leaving home in the morning and on returning home at evening congratulated themselves for having survived another day. Because of his peasant origins and his early life as a monk and rebel, and perhaps particularly because of his personal ugliness and the fact that his surname and the Chinese word for pig are pronounced identically, T'ai-tsu developed paranoidal suspicions of the associates who helped him win the throne, of the scholar-officials whom he brought into his service, and of the well-to-do in general. He exterminated his subordinates in a series of fanatical purges that kept the Ming officialdom intimidated and awed in its relations with the throne thereafter.

Governmental structure. The form of government initiated by T'ai-tsu and consolidated by Ch'eng-tsu, who was less tyrannical but equally autocratic, placed in the emperor's hands more centralized power than any previous native ruler had exercised. General administration was carried on by the traditional six ministries, but after 1380 they were directly coordinated by the emperor without the intervention of a chief councilor or prime minister. Military command was fragmented among five Chief Military Commissions, also coordinated solely by the emperor. In the central government only the surveillance function was left undivided, under the traditional Censorate. Provincial-level authority was split three ways, among a Provincial Administration Office, a Provincial Surveillance Office, and a Regional Military Commission in each of the 13 provinces into which China Proper was now organized.

The inescapable need for coordinating agencies soon led to the emergence at court of a new institution, a Grand Secretariat consisting of nonadministrators drawn from the venerable Hanlin Academy; these came to serve as paperwork aides and advisers for emperors without having the powers of T'ang or Sung chief councilors. For provincial-level supervision, the central government began delegating Grand Coordinators and, eventually, multi-province Supreme Commanders; but such dignitaries were provincial governors and regional viceroys only in embryo. At a lower level, as in Sung times, various types of circuit intendants were detached from provincial agencies to coordinate matters between the provincial and prefectural administrations.

By the early 1400's, as shown in the accompanying chart, the Ming government had developed a centralized, stable, well-articulated structure.

Civil service. The civil officialdom was recruited basically in the late Sung pattern and, however humbled by the autocratic Ming emperors, was more prestigious in society and more dominant in routine administration than ever. After the earliest Ming decades no one gained prominence in government without having been recruited in open, competitive examinations leading to the coveted chin-shih degree. To a greater extent than in earlier times, the examinations regularly brought into government men without prominent forebears.

During most of the dynasty the government functioned effectively enough: a series of grand secretaries, by collaborating with influential palace eunuchs, managed to keep things going despite the impetuosity or indolence of emperors on one hand and, on the other, an officialdom that did not consider the grand secretaries its natural leaders and spokesmen and was always inclined to think the worst of eunuchs. Eunuchs in Ming times often did take abusive advantage of their opportunities to influence emperors, but the officialdom regularly produced bold remonstrators who exercised some restraints on aberrant emperors. The most famous remonstrator was Hai Jui (1514–87). When he delivered at the palace a denunciation of Shih-tsung's (r. 1521–67) Taoist idiosyncrasies, the emperor ordered in a rage that he not be permitted to escape. "Never fear, sire," the eunuch go-between responded. "He has said goodbye to his family, has brought his coffin with him, and waits at the gate!" Shih-

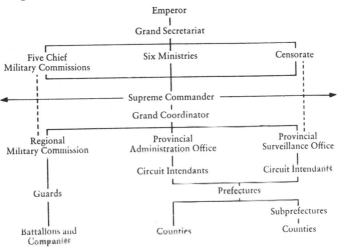

Basic governmental organization in Ming times

tsung was so taken aback that he decided to overlook Hai's impertinence.

The military. The Ming military system was an innovation intended to be self-supporting and self-perpetuating. Men in service at the beginning of the dynasty were designated a permanent, hereditary standing army. Soldiers were settled in garrisons, where they were required to farm as well as engage in basic military training. In rotation, they were called up for intensive training in the capital guards or for defense duty along the Great Wall and in other posts. When a special campaign was organized, troops serving in the capital guards were detached to the commands of generals in charge, appointed by the emperor through the civil service Ministry of War. Soldiers' families, exempted from various state obligations, were called on for replacements when men grew old or died in service. T'ai-tsu boasted, in what was clearly an exaggeration, that he mustered 1,000,000 men without imposing any cost at all on the civilian population.

The Long Ming Stability

Social leveling. One thing that contributed to the some-what lackluster character of Ming China was a dramatic social leveling attempted by T'ai-tsu. The new regime delib-erately catered to the poor and humbled the rich. Slavery was abolished, and large estates were confiscated by the state. State-claimed lands, beyond those needed for military garri-sons, were then rented out to the landless, who were also offered seeds, tools, farm animals, and tax incentives to resettle the long-depressed and underpopulated regions of the north. Inordinately high tax rates were imposed on the rich and cultured southeastern area between the Yangtze River and Hangchow, and thousands of wealthy southeastern families were forcibly resettled elsewhere, especially in the original dynastic capital at Nanking. Because T'ai-tsu had little faith in the good sense of the educated class of literati from whom he had to recruit his officials, he entrusted the assessment, collection, and forwarding of land taxes to the rural communities themselves, and he required villages to organize themselves for various kinds of local self-govern-ment. At times he even forbade county magistrates to travel into the countryside surrounding their county seats. More than any previous Chinese ruler, T'ai-tsu also fostered ele-mentary schooling throughout the empire. In consequence of all these policies, though the gap between rich and poor was by no means closed, the trend of early Ming life was toward a somewhat populist mediocrity. The trend was accentuated by the national need to reestablish a stable normalcy—to restore order and rebuild after the long age of nomad disruptions.

Isolationism and conservatism. In the same spirit, the early Ming expansionism was coupled with a xenophobic isola-tionism. Chinese were forbidden to have contacts with foreigners except on state business or under close state supervision, as if Chinese civilization had to be protected from contamination by outsiders. The Ming mood thus contrasted sharply with the cosmopolitan openness of the T'ang era. Tributary missions from foreign rulers were subjected to limitations and restraints, and the international trade that had been growing for centuries, especially in the southern ports, was severely curtailed. Soon after Ch'eng-tsu's reign the great overseas naval expeditions were terminated. The court abandoned its efforts to keep the troublesome Vietnamese subdued and in 1428 acquiesced in the restoration of their independence. Trade relations more satisfactory to the proud Japanese were negotiated. Ming garrisons were withdrawn from Inner Mongolia, and the Great Wall was rebuilt into the impressive monument it remains today, more formidable than ever before. Even the pretense of Chinese military domination of Central Asia lapsed. Though China by no means cowered within its frontiers, its attitude toward outsiders became decidedly defensive, and the military establishment began a long decline. Since the beginning of the dynasty it had been equipped with crude cannons that were admittedly dangerous to use, as early Western cannons were. In the late 1400's, when a touring censorial inspector demanded that one garrison's obviously neglected cannons be fired in a demonstration, the commander exclaimed in alarm, "Fire those things? Why, they might kill somebody!"

The mood of fifteenth-century intellectuals was equally unadventuresome. As one philosopher expressed it, "Since the time of Chu Hsi the Way has been clearly known. There is no more need for writing; what is left for us is to practice." Conservative, practical conformism was the order of the day.

The Chinese enjoyed stable peace for nearly two centuries. The government was occasionally embarrassed by Mongol raiders—especially when the chieftain Esen in 1449 captured the emperor Ying-tsung (r. 1435–49 and 1457–64) and demanded a huge ransom. On that occasion, the central government simply refused to pay, installed a brother as successor emperor, and strengthened its defenses, so that Esen eventually gave Ying-tsung back to be rid of the bother of keeping him in luxurious captivity. In the last half of the sixteenth century both Mongols and waves of coastal raiders from Japan were regular irritants; but the government learned to cope with such annoyances by appeasement and artful diplomacy as much as by arms.

Sixteenth-Century Vitality

North China slowly recovered from its long political and economic depression, though it was not to regain either demographic or economic parity with the south until the twentieth century. The Chinese population as a whole, from an early Ming level of less than 60,000,000, swelled beyond 100,000,000 and possibly closer to 200,000,000 by 1600. After the initial Ming agrarian-oriented retrenchment, which lasted through most of the fifteenth century, urban and commercial growth resumed. This combined with ever-spreading education to produce a lively, affluent bourgeois atmosphere in the sixteenth century. The great cities of the lower Yangtze region—Nanking, Soochow, and Hangchow especially—became renowned centers of textile and other manufacturing, interregional trade, publishing, intellectual and cultural life, and popular entertainment.

Culture. Ming intellectuals, associating in multitudes of private academies, produced monuments of scholarship, reams of all the traditional types of poetry, and paintings in both the academic (flowers and birds) and literati (bamboo and expressionistic monochrome landscapes) traditions. By the end of the sixteenth century painting handbooks were circulating that made it possible for everyone with the least skill to paint landscapes in the respectable amateurish fashion, "by the book"; but a great painter, Tung Ch'i-ch'ang (1555-1636), was proclaiming that only the disciplined, cultured man was capable of expressing anything of value, and that he did so by expressing inner truth in simple abstractions—not sentimentality and not prettiness—through the integrity of his brushstrokes. State and private kilns, especially inland from Hangchow at Ching-te-chen, produced thousands of handsome blue-and-white porcelain bowls, cups, jars, and vases, and then turned out wares that were even more decorative, with enameled glazes in three and finally five colors.

Literature. For the bourgeoisie, Ming playwrights refined the Yuan theatrical traditions and produced long-drawn-out operas with new, livelier musical scores. Long-popular story-tellers' tales, especially the erotic ones, were collected by connoisseurs, edited, and published in vernacular language. The development of colloquial fiction culminated in a series of long novels by obscure or unidentifiable authors that are now recognized in retrospect as literary classics, though disdained by most of the Ming educated elite, at least publicly, as being too vulgar for any reader of refinement. They especially include the following, each of which was a model for many subsequent publications in a similar genre:

1. *Romance of the Three Kingdoms (San-kuo chih yen-i),* a fictionalized history of the late Han and immediate post-Han years.

2. *Water Margin (Shui-hu chuan,* also known in translation as *All Men Are Brothers),* a picaresque, Robin Hood–like novel of violence and adventure.

3. *The Record of a Journey to the West (Hsi-yu chi,* known in translation as *Monkey),* a supernatural and wildly humorous fable about the travels of a T'ang Buddhist pilgrim to India, escorted by a bumbling pig and a magic-working scamp of a monkey, who is perhaps the best-known fictional creation in all Chinese literature.

4. *Chin P'ing Mei* (known in one translation as *Golden Lotus),* a masterpiece of pornographic satire about the amorous adventures of a pharmacist with his six wives and a

bevy of other women, including his own maidservants and his neighbors' wives, which provides a panoramic view of six-teenth-century Chinese society peopled by believable men and women.

Wang Yang-ming. In philosophy the conservative Neo-Confucianism of Chu Hsi was now challenged dramatically by Wang Yang-ming (or Wang Shou-jen; 1472–1529), who was one of the foremost litterateurs and officials of his time, once serving as supreme commander in supervisory control of five provinces in the south. From his background as a profound thinker who also had considerable experience in government, Wang devised the concept, influential into the twentieth century, that knowledge and action are an insep-arable unity—that only disciplined theory can lead to effec-tive action, and theory can be tested only in application. More important, he disagreed with Chu Hsi's notion that cosmic principles (li) can be understood only through exten-sive study. In an experience akin to the sudden enlightenment sought by Ch'an Buddhists, it came to Wang after years of study that all principles exist in every man's mind, in much the same sense that Mencius anciently spoke of the seeds of virtue being part of man's natural endowment. Wang taught fascinated disciples that true principles are expressed in the natural, spontaneous impulses of the individual mind.

In the late sixteenth century Wang's teachings were exaggerated by what was known as the "mad Ch'an" school. Its followers proclaimed that every man is his own judge of right and wrong, that every impulse should be translated unthinkingly into action, and that "the streets are full of sages." They preached egalitarian, libertarian doctrines to large, excited crowds in the towns and cities, giving philo-sophical justification to a popular habit of accepting Confu-cian, Taoist, and Buddhist doctrines equally. The extremism of the "mad Ch'an" movement offended many scholar-officials. By the end of the dynasty the heyday of Wang's "school of mind" individualism was over, and conservative, conformist Chu Hsi-ism remained dominant in Chinese philosophy.

The Ming Decline

The later Ming emperors were as capricious as their predecessors, and increasingly withdrawn. Shih-tsung (or Chia-ching; r. 1521–67) and Shen-tsung (or Wan-li; r. 1572–1620) both isolated themselves for decades from direct contact with their ministers. Grand secretaries and palace eunuchs, trying to keep the government functioning, aroused endless partisan wrangling in the officialdom, which made the government increasingly unresponsive to social problems and encouraged emperors to become increasingly truculent. Declining governmental effectiveness came to a climax in the 1620's, when a young and indecisive emperor gave almost dictatorial power to the most notorious palace eunuch of all Chinese history, Wei Chung-hsien (1568–1627). Wei brutally purged hundreds of officials associated with a conservative reformist group called the Tung-lin Party, and staffed the government with sycophants.

Meantime, the state treasury had been seriously depleted and the military establishment weakened by a long war in the 1590's, in which China helped its vassal Korea to survive an invasion by the Japanese military dictator Toyotomi Hideyoshi. The hereditary soldiers were by now largely incompetent pensioners and had to be supplemented with recruited mercenaries and civilian conscripts. Moreover, the late Ming affluence had a shaky foundation. Technological progress was not keeping pace with population growth and urbanization—perhaps because of bureaucratic conservatism among officials, who with their relatives and hangers-on now dominated commerce. Also, the exploitation of tax breaks and other advantages by the elite gradually undermined the free peasantry of early Ming times, so that tenancy became increasingly widespread. The late Ming affluence, in short, was neither self-perpetuating nor equitably distributed.

Deterioration in governmental morale and widespread economic discontent coincided with two serious threats to national stability: a domestic rebellion in the severely depressed northwest and the consolidation of an antagonistic Manchu regime in the northeast. One such threat might have been contained, but the government could not cope with both at once. The domestic rebel Li Tzu-ch'eng (1605?–45) captured Peking in 1644, whereupon the last Ming emperor hanged himself in the palace grounds. A frontier general invited the Manchus to join him in putting down the rebels, and the Manchus seized the opportunity to take the throne for themselves.

While Ming China had been basking in its inward-oriented self-satisfaction and remained supremely confident of its cultural superiority over all "barbarian" peoples, the states of Western Europe were embarking on their great age of exploration, colonization, and imperialism. In 1498 Vasco da Gama rounded South Africa and reached India. In 1511 the Portuguese conquered Malacca, which controlled access from the Indian Ocean to the South China Sea; and in 1514 a Portuguese squadron appeared at Canton seeking diplomatic and trading relations. Although discouraged by the Ming court, the Portuguese persevered and by 1557 had a permanent settlement on China's coast at Macao. From there Jesuit missionaries penetrated inland, and in 1601 Matteo Ricci was permitted to establish a Catholic missionary headquarters at Peking under imperial patronage. By the end of Ming other Europeans had also begun to make contact with China. The Chinese attitude toward them all was one of patronizing tolerance at best.

Ch'ing

The alien Manchus who in 1644 inaugurated the last imperial dynasty in China, Ch'ing (1644–1912), were related to the Jurchen whose Chin dynasty had ruled North China from 1127 to 1234. The national name Manchu, of unclear derivation and significance, was adopted late, in 1636. Through most of the Ming dynasty these northern tribes had been forest-dwelling vassals of the Chinese in far eastern Manchuria. They were troublesome enough at times to cause Ming authorities to build defensive palisades against them around the Chinese settlements in the Liao River basin. But they eventually became avid admirers and students of Chinese civilization, and when they took control of China it was their contention that they came, not as despoilers, but as preservers of the Ming heritage. And as a matter of fact, their rule over their Chinese subjects was by far the least burdensome of any imposed on the Chinese by aliens.

The Era of Transition

The Manchus owed their nationhood to two organizing geniuses, Nurhachi (1559–1626) and his son Abahai (1592–1643). Nurhachi began life as a petty tribal chief who sold medicinal herbs to Chinese settlers in Manchuria and led tributary missions to Peking. Abahai died as emperor of a strong, effective Ch'ing dynasty headquartered at Mukden that dominated Mongolia and Korea as well as all of Manchuria and confronted Ming China's finest army at Shan-hai-kuan, where the Great Wall meets the sea. When Li Tzu-ch'eng's rebels, after capturing Peking, moved northeast toward Shan-hai-kuan in 1644 the Ming commander there, Wu San-kuei (1612–78), and the Manchu prince regent, Dorgon (1612–50), collaborated against them as friendly enemies. Li's forces, badly routed, fell back to Peking, looted the city, and then fled westward. Wu San-kuei's army and mixed Chinese-Manchu forces scattered to destroy Li and restore order in China. Promising Wu princely status and a large fief, Dorgon then enthroned his nephew at Peking as the Shun-chih emperor (Shih-tsu, r. 1644–61).

The transition from Ming to Ch'ing rule was far less traumatic for the Chinese than the thirteenth-century Mongol conquest had been; indeed, it was the least disruptive transition from one major dynasty to another in the whole of

Chinese history. This was so despite the fact that, having won
the Chinese throne easily, almost as if by default, the new
Ch'ing dynasty took nearly half a century to secure its control
of the empire. Two things eased the transition. First, the
Manchus honored and perpetuated the Ming ideology, governmental patterns, and social organization; and second—in
one of the remarkable ironies of Chinese history—Ming
loyalists were overwhelmed as much by Chinese fighting in
the Manchu cause as by the Manchus themselves, even with
their Mongol allies.

In the earliest years of the Manchu uprising in the
northeast, many Chinese settlers in Manchuria and defectors
from defeated Ming punitive expeditions willingly accepted
Manchu leadership because of their aversion to the partisan
squabbling at the Ming court and their disgust with the
ineptitude of the Ming military effort. The Manchus were not
anti-Chinese; they gladly incorporated Chinese defectors
into their socio-military groups, called banners, and gave
competent Chinese positions of responsibility. Later, when
the Manchus occupied North China with the help of Wu San-
kuei and other former Ming commanders, they introduced
themselves as liberators from chaos rather than oppressive
conquerors, and many Chinese welcomed them as such after
the instability of the last Ming decades.

Once the rebels of the north were suppressed, Chinese
armies under Wu San-kuei and other Chinese generals were
instrumental in destroying Ming loyalist regimes in the south.
Without such Chinese support, the Manchus would undoubtedly have been content to divide the country with a Southern
Ming regime, as the Jurchen had divided it with Southern
Sung. There was some prospect that such a division would
come about in any event, for the southern loyalists resisted
vigorously despite a continuation of the partisan wrangling
that had paralyzed the court at Peking. Four undistinguished
princes were successively installed by Ming generals in the
south, and it was not until 1662 that the last of them, having

taken refuge in Burma, was handed over by the king of Burma to an invading Ch'ing force under Wu San-kuei, who executed him.

Even then resistance was maintained on the offshore islands of the southeast coast by the family of a famous loyalist freebooter named Cheng Ch'eng-kung (1624–62; known to Europeans as Koxinga), who had established himself on Taiwan. At one point the Ch'ing government went so far as to order the whole southeastern coastline evacuated to deprive the Cheng raiders of looting possibilities. Moreover, Wu San-kuei and some other Ming defectors, after having been rewarded with large and almost autonomous fiefs in the south, turned against the Manchus in 1673 in what is known as the Rebellion of the Three Feudatories. For a time the rebels dominated almost the whole of South China. But in 1681 resistance on the mainland was finally crushed—ironically again, in large part by a new generation of Chinese generals serving the Ch'ing dynasty. Then, in 1683, the government mounted an invasion of Taiwan that finally quelled the Cheng family's coastal harassments. Thereafter nationalistic anti-Manchu sentiments were kept alive by secret societies, which now began to thrive in the fashion of the underworld gangs of the modern West, and by members of some of the large overseas Chinese communities that had developed in Southeast Asian countries in the last Ming century. But these rumblings of discontent were more irritants than threats, and in the 1680's the Manchus stabilized their control of the Chinese empire.

Early Ch'ing Prestige and Prosperity

The prolonged Ming loyalist resistance served to reinforce the Manchus' original inclination to deal prudently with the Chinese. They publicly honored the many men and women who had become martyrs in the Ming cause; they refrained from punishing eminent intellectuals who refused to enter their service; they tolerated a minor cult of Southern Ming historiography; they sought Chinese cooperation in many flattering ways. Into the eighteenth century there prevailed what some historians have called a Manchu-Chinese honeymoon.

For the first century and a half of their rule the Manchus gave China good government and strong leadership, so that Chinese life flourished in every regard. In the eighteenth century China attained the last golden age of the imperial tradition and very likely was the most awe-inspiring state in the world. It enjoyed a long domestic peace while steadily strengthening its preeminence over neighboring peoples; it grew in population and wealth and was elegantly sophisticated. Carrying on the lively traditions of the sixteenth century moderated by Chu Hsi-ist conservatism in philosophy, the Chinese elite produced enormous compilations of classical and historical scholarship, often under state auspices; wrote more and more poems and essays emulating the styles of past masters; and turned out painting after painting in the amateurish literati landscape style ordained by Tung Ch'i-ch'ang. Two more great vernacular novels appeared: (a) *An Unofficial History of the Confucian Literati (Ju-lin wai-shih,* known in translation simply as *The Scholars),* full of good-humored ridicule of the scholar-official class, by Wu Ching-tzu (1701–54); and (b) *Dream of the Red Chamber (Hung-lou meng),* a panoramic tale about the decline of an elegantly degenerate great family, by Ts'ao Hsüeh-ch'in (1724?–64). China's traditional principles of governance and social organization were so extolled by Voltaire and other Western intellectuals that Confucius became virtually the patron saint of Europe's Age of Enlightenment. A popular passion for Chinese things and themes (chinoiserie) had lasting influence on European art, literature, architecture, gardens, and decor. Much of the credit for such Chinese prospering belongs to the remarkably able early Manchu rulers, especially two dynastic giants called K'ang-hsi and Ch'ien-lung.

K'ang-hsi

The K'ang-hsi emperor (Sheng-tsu, r. 1661–1722), enthroned at the age of seven, reigned over China longer than any emperor before him and was probably the most admirable ruler of the entire later imperial age. Conscientious, inquisitive, and indefatigable, he had awesome physical and mental powers. He was thoroughly Chinese by culture, wrote literary prose and poetry of good quality, and encouraged literature, art, fine printing, and porcelain manufacture. Under Jesuit tutelage he studied Latin, higher mathematics, science, and the new Western technology; he was especially enamored of clocks and collected them with a connoisseur's relish. He corresponded with European kings and popes, but late in life he became irritated by the sectarian bickerings of Catholic missionaries and what he considered the outrageous presumption that a pope in Rome should determine what Chinese Christians could and could not believe.

A careful, frugal, and efficient administrator, the K'ang-hsi emperor made strenuous efforts to ensure honesty in government and to foster Chinese-Manchu harmony. He made six grand tours of inspection around the country to see for himself what conditions were like. He honored Chinese scholars and employed them in the production of dictionaries, encyclopedias, and other scholarship, as well as in routine civil service administration. He also watched carefully over the economy and fostered water-control projects that kept agriculture flourishing.

No less than in the domestic realm, the K'ang-hsi emperor was a determined and masterly leader in military affairs. While still a youth he boldly challenged the autonomy of Wu San-kuei and other powerful Chinese generals who had been enfeoffed in the south in the earliest Ch'ing years. In the resulting Rebellion of the Three Feudatories, he personally planned the campaigns that suppressed the rebels and subjugated Taiwan. In the midst of these exertions the eastern

Mongols (known as Tatars and Khalkas) revolted in the north, in 1675. The emperor reacted unhesitatingly, subdued them, and declared himself khan of all the Mongols. Subsequently the western Mongol chief Galdan (1632?–97) invaded Mongolia from Central Asia. The emperor personally led three campaigns northward in the 1690's, forced Galdan to commit suicide in 1697, and established military colonies at the Central Asian oases of Hami and Turfan. Further, by diplomatic intrigues he got an anti-Mongol Dalai Lama installed as ruler of Tibet. When Galdan's successors conquered Tibet in 1717, the emperor mounted expeditions that by 1720 had driven the Mongols out and made Tibet a submissive political appendage of China.

In the 1600's the Russians had completed the early stage of their eastward expansion across Siberia to the Pacific, and during the K'ang-hsi era they established outposts along the Amur River. Considering this Manchu territory, the emperor sent a Ch'ing army to attack the Russians' stronghold, Fort Albazin, in 1685–86. The Russians withdrew. In 1689 the Chinese and Russians negotiated China's first treaty with a European nation, the Treaty of Nerchinsk. The Russians gave up any claims to the Amur River valley. Border trade was authorized, and a long era of Sino-Russian peace ensued.

The K'ang-hsi emperor was succeeded by his fourth son, the Yung-cheng emperor (Shih-tsung, r. 1722–35), a man of forty-five. Because he came to the throne by intriguing successfully against his brothers, he was a wary ruler, harsher than his father; and he increased the autocratic quality of Ch'ing governance. But he was an able emperor who reinforced bureaucratic discipline and vigorously suppressed budding corruption.

Ch'ien-lung

His successor, the Ch'ien-lung emperor (Kao-tsung, r. 1735–96), retired after a 60-year reign so as not to exceed his grandfather's record but continued to dominate the government in retirement until his death in 1799, at the age of eighty-nine. He was a more flamboyant man than his predecessors, a Grand Monarch in the style of his contemporary, Louis XIV of France. But he was also a serious man, and like the K'ang-hsi emperor, was probably the most capable ruler anywhere in his time. Domestically, he generally continued in his grandfather's footsteps, and was an especially notable patron of monumental collaborative scholarly undertakings. In his time all forms of literature and art flourished, and China's prosperity seemed boundless. As the population grew and agriculture was intensified, new market towns sprang up in the countryside by the hundreds. Regional and national marketing complexes grew, generating new urban-oriented occupations and attitudes. The well-to-do began abandoning rural life to settle in the cities and concentrate on mercantile activity; and the peasantry, now a complicated mixture of part owners, part tenants, part small landlords, became increasingly sensitive to the fluctuating market needs in the towns and cities. China exuded self-confidence and self-satisfaction.

The Ch'ien-lung emperor was proudest of his military achievements, for which he had a great flair. He pursued an aggressive policy of dominating troublesome border peoples. The western Mongols (called Eleuthes, Kalmuks, or Dzungars) were still the most troublesome neighbors. After rebelling repeatedly in the 1720's and 1730's, they ceded the eastern end of Turkestan to Ch'ing in 1735. But they continued to make trouble until the 1750's, when in a series of campaigns the Ch'ien-lung emperor completely destroyed Mongol power in Central Asia. The whole of Chinese Turkestan was then incorporated directly into the Ch'ing empire in 1759, with its modern name Sinkiang (New Dominion). A few years earlier, in 1751, an expedition had established Ch'ing control of Tibet more tightly than before, in reaction to renewed unrest. Later, in 1792, a Ch'ing army in Tibet marched southward into Nepal to punish Gurka tribesmen who had long encroached on and pillaged parts of Tibet, and Nepal was forced to recognize Ch'ing suzerainty. Ch'ing armies also campaigned extensively in southwestern China, whose aboriginal tribes did not fully succumb to Ch'ing authority until 1776. Burma and northern Vietnam suffered from Ch'ing punitive expeditions in 1765–69 and 1788, respectively, but retained their independence, as tributary vassals.

The glory of the Ch'ien-lung emperor's reign is blemished seriously by two things. One is an extensive literary inquisition that was begun in the 1770's, aimed at suppressing subversive sentiments. The other is the personal deterioration of the emperor himself in his later years. He gradually became extravagant and luxury-loving, began to surround himself with docile sycophants, and finally, from about 1775 to his death, was the dupe of a clever, unscrupulous Manchu guardsman named Ho-shen (1750–99). Handsome and amusing, Ho-shen swiftly rose from an obscure post in the imperial bodyguard into the highest ministerships, attained lavish honors, and systematically exploited every possibility of bribery and other forms of corruption. The cumulative result of the literary inquisition and Ho-shen's pernicious influence was that in the final Ch'ien-lung years the Ch'ing government began a rapid decline in morale and effectiveness.

Pressures from the West

Two major types of pressures hastened the deterioration of the imperial tradition in the nineteenth century. One was the increasing power and ambition of the West. By 1800 the English, Dutch, Spanish, French, and Portuguese had developed colonial empires in Asia, and the newly independent Americans were brandishing free-trade doctrines around the world. Yet for almost three centuries China—the most populous, wealthiest, and by Western reckoning most powerful country on earth—had resisted and carefully limited its contacts with the West. Insignificant overland trade with

Russia was tolerated, but seafaring Westerners were permitted to trade only at Canton, only in trading seasons defined by the Chinese, only with a licensed monopoly of Chinese wholesalers (called by Westerners the *co-hong*), and only under close state supervision. Moreover, whereas the West clamored for such Chinese products as tea, silk, and porcelains, the Chinese had little use for any Western products, so that Western silver poured endlessly into Chinese coffers.

By about 1800, however, Westerners found they could sell opium to the Chinese in abundance, even if illegally; and gradually the trade imbalance was righted in this way. By the 1830's the Canton trading situation had reversed itself: opium was pouring in and silver was pouring out. The Ch'ing government, alarmed both by the silver drain and by the spread of opium-smoking, tried to regain control of the situation and finally provoked the leading trading country, England, into war. The so-called Opium War of 1839–42, though not fought very vigorously by either side and limited for the most part to coastal skirmishes, went badly for China. To avoid more serious humiliation the Ch'ing court made peace with England, and soon negotiated treaties with other trading nations, on such terms that China became exposed to still more contacts with the rude, importunate "foreign devils." A total of five ports, from Canton to Shanghai, were opened to regular foreign residence as well as trade. Foreign influences of many sorts began making themselves felt in the interior, to the great dismay of the Ch'ing authorities.

Domestic Pressures

Growing domestic discontent was a more ominous problem for nineteenth-century China. The population had grown steadily since mid-Ming times—to more than 300,000,-000 by 1750 and 400,000,000 by 1850. Increasing food production—partly due to the spread of new subsidiary crops introduced from the Americas, including maize, potatoes, and peanuts—made such growth possible; but land utilization had reached its peak in the eighteenth century, even with China's very high level of premodern agricultural technology. Population growth inevitably surpassed increased food production, and the standard of living began to decline. Spreading corruption and indolence in government made conditions worse. For the first time in history there appeared a permanently dispossessed class of impoverished people for whom there were neither lands nor jobs, and their numbers could only multiply.

The rumblings of anti-Manchu secret societies became more threatening every year. The centuries-old White Lotus Society, a Buddhist group, ignited a rebellion in 1793 that disrupted North China until 1804. Then in the 1820's and 1830's popular uprisings became endemic. The government's humiliation in the Opium War weakened its prestige, its confidence, and its general ability to cope with its mushrooming domestic problems. Finally, in 1850, South China erupted in what is called the Taiping Rebellion, which for the next 15 years shook the Ch'ing dynasty almost but not quite to its destruction. More than 15 provinces were affected, hundreds of towns and cities were damaged or destroyed, and an estimated 30,000,000 lives were lost. The very foundations of the traditional imperial system—its basic political principles and patterns of social organization—were challenged as never before.

The Old Order in Distress

Contemporaries both inside and outside China were slow to recognize the fact, but in retrospect it is clear that with the outbreak of the Taiping Rebellion, following close upon the impact of the Opium War, traditional Chinese civilization in all its aspects plunged into a transition unlike any experienced before. China's modern history was beginning, and it was to prove a traumatic process of reorientation and reidentification.

The agonies China has experienced since 1850 found rebels

and warlords, last-ditch dynasts and republican revolution-
aries, moderates and radicals pitted against each other in
successive waves of struggle either to preserve the status
quo at any cost or to keep struggling toward new political institutions, new ideologies, and new patterns of socioeconomic organization that might restore the stability,
prosperity, cultural flowering, and international esteem that
China enjoyed in the best times of its long past. The process
has been prolonged and difficult in large part because the old
order, despite its autumnal splendor in the eighteenth century, was in severe distress by the middle of the nineteenth
century. Among its noteworthy disabilities were the following:

1. China was ruled by aliens. Notwithstanding the Manchus' championship of traditional Chineseness, they were
after all not Chinese; and their determination to preserve the
Chinese heritage as the means of safeguarding their predominance made them feel all the more threatened by the changes
that were now required of China—more threatened than
native rulers might have felt.

2. The banner military organization upon which Manchu
predominance had been built was now, like the Ming hereditary soldiery in the 1600's, so deteriorated that the dynasty
had to rely for its support on Chinese militiamen, mercenaries, and local defense forces, among whom there was little
sense of loyalty to the throne and scarcely more of nationalistic patriotism.

3. Nothing in China's experience prepared it to appreciate what had been happening in the West since 1600 or the
mentality of the Western merchants, missionaries, and mili-
tarists who now clamored for ever more attention. The
ritualistic protocol of the millenniums-old tributary system,
rooted in the conviction that China's moral and cultural
superiority would prevail in the end against the aggressive-
ness of any "foreign devils," hardly suited the country's new
need to deal with outsiders whose technological, economic,

and organizational advantages placed it in the unfamiliar, unthinkable position of a relatively primitive have-not nation in a world of many nations dedicated to competition rather than harmony.

4. The administrative mechanisms and the ideology that had served China's domestic purposes well since 1400, on balance, were no longer adequate. The ratio of chin-shih degrees to all males, which had been 1 : 250,000 in Sung times and 1 : 500,000 in Ming times, had plummeted to about 1 : 2,000,000. As a result, the ordinary man's hope that with hard work and good luck he or one of his sons might succeed in the civil service recruitment examinations and thus win prestige, power, and wealth—the Chinese equivalent of the American log cabin to White House dream—had faded entirely away. Conversely, whereas in Sung times a county magistrate was responsible for a population of 80,000 on average, his late Ch'ing counterpart was responsible for 250,000, so that the social distance separating the empire's officials and the general populace had spread to such an extent that the ordinary man was unlikely ever to see an official, much less know of any family that had produced one. The traditional saying that "Heaven is high, and the emperor is far away" was no longer enough; officials themselves were now almost as remote from the populace as emperors had once been, and as insulated from the harsh realities of ordinary life.

5. Civil service officials in consequence were no longer the natural leaders of society, which had been their role in Sung, Ming, and even early Ch'ing times. They were tainted by being the willing servants of alien and increasingly embattled rulers. Their bookish, moralistic training and outlook and their status as the most privileged group in the population made it all but impossible for them to appreciate the problems or to cope with the changes that were engulfing China. Moreover, the management void created by the increasing remoteness of the regular officialdom from the

general populace was now filled by hireling clerks and tax agents, opportunistic townsmen, and miscellaneous local notables, from among whom it was hardly likely that a promising new leadership might emerge. China was threatened with the prospect of wallowing in leaderless stagnation.

6. Long accustomed to national security, social stability, a proud high culture, and a reasonably equitable level of general welfare, the Chinese had not felt impelled to embark on exploitative adventures abroad or otherwise to transform themselves in the innovative ways that brought about mercantilism, imperialism, and the Industrial Revolution in the West. China had basked too long in its traditionalistic self-contentment when, in the 1800's, change suddenly became imperative; and then it was too late for anything less than drastic change. The old order, it might be argued, had been too successful for its own good.

China's struggle out of the morass of troubles' into which the traditional civilization had drifted by 1850, though one of the more fascinating themes of modern world history, is not properly part of this present tale. Our story fades out in the ashes of the old order, from which a new order is gradually rising, phoenix-like, characterized by a different but still unique Chineseness.

INDEX